"Andy Epstein has written a bible for every designer working in or with a corporation. It is insightful, revealing, and provocative, and a must-read for anyone looking to make a difference—and an impact—with design."

—**Debbie Millman**, President, AIGA;
President, Sterling Brands

"Intelligent, practical, and honest with the perfect amount of humor. Chock full of valuable information, sound business principles and real-world ideas on bringing creativity back into the corporate environment. Andy covers *everything* unique to in-house design teams including client impressions, staff resources, and most importantly being true to yourself."

—**Jeni Herberger**, Principal, Design Matters Inc; Co-founder and President, Big Fish

"Any designer who has ever worked in-house will instantly recognize the truth of what Andy Epstein presents in this book. It is both insightful and practical, and should be required reading for anyone who manages a creative team or department. Consider it a manual for building and maintaining a sustainable creative group that will provide value to its corporation."

—**Andy Brenits**, Vice President, InSource;
Visiting Professor, Pratt Institute;
Associate Director, NDPPS, KPMG LLP

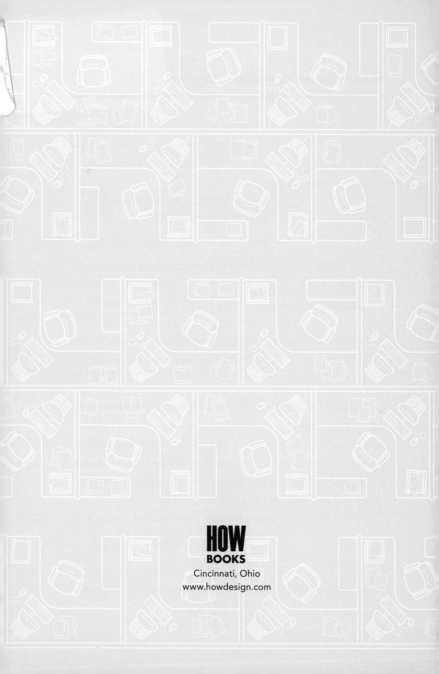

HOW
BOOKS
Cincinnati, Ohio
www.howdesign.com

THE CORPORATE
CREATIVE

tips and tactics for thriving as an in-house designer

ANDY EPSTEIN

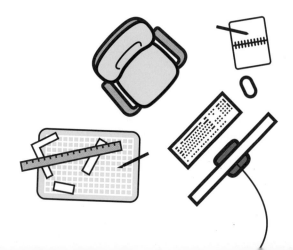

For more excellent books and resources for designers, visit www.how design.com.

14 13 12 11 10   5 4 3 2 1

Distributed in Canada by Fraser Direct, 100 Armstrong Avenue, Georgetown, Ontario, Canada L7G 5S4, Tel: (905) 877-4411. Distributed in the U.K. and Europe by David & Charles, Brunel House, Newton Abbot, Devon, TQ12 4PU, England, Tel: (+44) 1626-323200, Fax: (+44) 1626-323319, E-mail: postmaster@davidandcharles.co.uk. Distributed in Australia by Capricorn Link, P.O. Box 704, Windsor, NSW 2756 Australia, Tel: (02) 4577-3555.

Library of Congress Cataloging-in-Publication Data

Epstein, Andy.
 The corporate creative / Andy Epstein.
     p. cm.
 Includes index.
 ISBN 978-1-60061-418-7 (pbk. : alk. paper)
 1. Creative ability in business. 2. Corporate culture. I. Title.
 HD53.E67 2010
 658.4'063--dc22
                                    2009043013

Edited by Amy Schell
Designed by Grace Ring
Production coordinated by Greg Nock

ACKNOWLEDGMENTS

I'd like to thank all of the designers I've had the privilege to meet and work with. In particular, I'd like to thank fellow design business thinkers Emily Cohen, Brad Weed, Stanley Hainsworth and Shel Perkins for their insights. Sincere thank yous to my mentors Jim Trusilo, Rick Buchanan, Mike Sheller and Myrna McGrath. A special call out to the ubiquitous three Andys—Peter Sheridan, Jim O'Brien and Scott Canady. In the greater design community, a number of individuals extended themselves and shared with me wonderful opportunities. They include Bryn Mooth, Megan Lane Patrick and the rest of the staff at HOW; Ric Grefé, David Hall and all the committed members of AIGA; and Glenn Arnowitz, Marty Shova, Robin Friedman (a special supporter) and the board at InSource. Extra special thanks to my personal editors and fan club—my mom and dad. Most importantly, I'd like to thank my wife and daughters, from whom I derive my most sublime joy and greatest lessons.

ABOUT THE AUTHOR

After graduating from Carnegie-Mellon university, Andy Epstein started his career as a freelance designer and illustrator working with clients including Bacardi, Canon, Bantam Books and Merck. Jumping into the world of in-house in 1992, Epstein created and expanded in-house design teams for Commonwealth Toy and Gund. He later restructured and expanded the hundred-person creative team at Bristol-Myers-Squibb and consulted at Johnson & Johnson. He currently works at Designer Greetings, leading an in-house design team that develops the company's card and gift wrap product lines. Epstein writes and speaks extensively on in-house issues, and is the co-founder of InSource, an association dedicated to providing support to in-house designers and design team managers. As head of the AIGA In-house Design task force, he is continuing his efforts to empower in-house teams and raise their stature in the design and business communities.

TABLE OF CONTENTS

I remember one time my team was particularly fired up about gaining a more strategic role in the company. They came to me hollering, "The only way we're going to have a seat at the table is if we storm the castle!" To which I responded, "You're already in the castle … Now what?"

— BRAD WEED
Partner Group Manager,
Microsoft

PROLOGUE

It's 1970; in a scene right out of *Dazed and Confused*, I sit in Ms. Powell's seventh-grade civics class jamming on an essay answer for a semester exam. I'm happy. I've studied hard for this test, and it seems to have paid off. Ms. Powell walks up and down the aisles in what she claims is an attempt to help us if she sees any of us hitting roadblocks. We all know she just wants to make sure we're not cheating.

I feel her slightly malevolent presence just behind me and I freeze up, forgetting the next point I was preparing to make. She leans over. She squints down at my test. She purses her lips and then clucks. I'm toast, and frantically I try to figure out what I did wrong.

She straightens up and derisively declares loud enough for the whole class to hear, "Andy, why do you always have to be different?"

I'm shocked, confused, embarrassed and angered all at the same time. What did I do that was different? The last thing a seventh grader wants is to be called out as different from his peers. I just want to fit in.

Ms. Powell proceeds to point out that my essay answer apparently had little if anything to do with the question. This is not uncommon for me. There are many times when I interpret a word or phrase differently from the way it was intended. This is not anything I do on purpose, but apparently, Ms. Powell thinks I do and takes it as a personal affront.

Fast forward to 2006. I head up a large creative department at Bristol-Myers Squibb (BMS). I've been told that of the almost one hundred positions on my team, most of which are filled with contract workers, sixty-six have to be converted to full-time positions—in three months. If you do the math and figure three to four interviews are needed per position, you end up with a heartburn-inducing 264 interviews in ninety days, or four interviews each work day.

Of course, we set up interview teams to divvy up the workload, but I end up on many of them. A few germane points—all of the contract workers currently in the sixty-six positions are applying for the full-time jobs, so I have worked for almost a year with all of them. They are interviewing for a wide variety of positions at all different management levels, from production artists to designers to design team managers. Most importantly, the interview process we are mandated by HR to use, Experience Based Interviews, requires that the interviewee recount, in some detail, past situations relating to a variety of topics including leadership, collaboration, innovation, etc. The assumption is that we can determine how the candidate would operate at BMS when confronted with situations similar to the ones they are asked to recount.

Even before we get into a half dozen interviews, it becomes clear that the candidates are struggling with the questions. They aren't answering the questions with any specificity; they digress and veer off into generalities and spout design platitudes. This occurs with all of the candidates regardless of their current positions, talents, skills and past professional experience. By the thirteenth or fourteenth interview, things are quickly deteriorating.

I'll never forget the breaking point. Jill White, our HR staffing specialist, and I interview Michael Liang, one of our most talented senior designers who has an amazing flair for creating branding campaigns. We ask Michael a question on leadership or some related topic, and he launches into a twenty minute diatribe that starts with Watergate and ends with a dissertation on string theory. At the close of the interview, after Michael proudly leaves the conference room, Jill practically jumps across the table, grabs me by the lapels, and plaintively asks me what the hell is going on. I am as dazed and frustrated as she is. I tell her I just don't know.

Over the next few days, I think about the interviews, and I start to recall incidents in my academic and professional career, like my experience with Ms. Powell. I see a pattern. Whenever I, or creatives like me, were forced to fit into an organization or process predicated on more verbal, linear, nonvisual and noncreative ways of thinking and behaving, we crashed and burned. I realize that the true challenge isn't even just getting through the damn interviews. It is that, as creatives working in the corporate environment, we have to deal with these disconnects and hurdles dozens of times a day, every day.

I believe that we in-house designers must figure out how to bridge these gaps yet maintain our individual gifts. Only then will we find true professional fulfillment and contribute to our companies fully and powerfully.

INTRODUCTION

There is no unique branch of design known as in-house design. There are no distinct design skills possessed solely by in-house designers. There are no special courses in design school for in-house design. There are no exclusive design or professional standards for in-house design. There are no fonts, applications, stock photos, hardware or software specifically created for in-house design. In-house design as some kind of different practice of design does not exist.

> What do exist are designers practicing design in corporations.

They are, from a pure design perspective, creating design artifacts using exactly the same skills and talents as their colleagues who are working in independent design firms or running their own small studios. In-house designers just happen to be designing in the corporate environment. This is how in-house design needs to be defined, because this is the only framework that allows internal creative teams the perspective needed to effectively address the professional challenges that they face.

That definition means this book has little or nothing to do with the actual act of creating design. There are plenty of books and authors much more capable than I to support you in that area. What this book does offer are ways to deal with the frustrating, mind-numbing, inspiration-killing, creativity-murdering, disheartening, demoralizing and demeaning challenges that working in a corporate environment can pose to creatives at their place of work each and every day.

Given these challenges, as an in-house designer you may be asking yourself why you choose to work in a company in the first place. Maybe you believe that this is the arena where, as a designer, you can truly have an impact by being afforded the opportunity to influence the marketing and design process in ways an outside vendor never could. Maybe you enjoy having access to greater resources, both in terms of equipment and human capital, than are available to independent designers. You may also want the security, better benefits, more stable hours and camaraderie of partnering with others that working in-house often provides.

Whatever the reason, the path you've chosen now requires you to behave and think in ways different from designers working outside of the corporate sphere. You need to acknowledge that you operate in a right-brain/left-brain world that requires you to be a project manager as well as a designer, a businessperson as well as a creative, both a visual and a verbal communicator. It's a fifty-fifty proposition.

Surviving and, more importantly, succeeding as a creative in the corporate environment is a balancing act between these extreme mindsets and ways of being that takes years of experience to perfect. It also requires compromise without selling out, discipline without the sacrifice of spontaneity and passion coupled with a controlled state of cool. You have to meet your corporate culture halfway but do so with integrity and honesty. Not everyone is cut out for this gig. For those who are, the world of in-house offers tremendous opportunities to effect real change on a large scale.

One caveat: In spite of the need to meet your company halfway and to strive to fit into its culture, it's important to always keep in mind that, as a creative, you really are different from your peers in the corporate world (as if you didn't already know that). You need to work with this reality, not resist it or abuse it, and leverage those differences to establish yourself and your teams as valuable players in the corporate world.

I propose you have even more to offer your companies than the creation of artifacts that sell, educate or inspire. You embody a way of being that is radically different from others in the corporate world and can positively impact the way your nondesign co-workers relate to each other, their managers and their work.

This book is designed to quickly hone in on key strategies and tactics to help you in your pursuit of establishing yourself and your team as powerful players in your company. Follow its tenets and you will be in a position to improve your situation in ways that will result in a more fulfilling, purposeful, professional life.

A special note: As in-house designers, we may believe that there should be dozens of books dedicated to the subject of in-house design, but the reality is that, while we are an important group within the larger design community, we are a relatively small subset nonetheless, and the possibility that numerous books will be published on the subject is pretty remote.

Therefore, when presented with the unique opportunity to write a book for our community, I chose to address the broadest in-house audience possible by speaking to both higher level management issues and topics that are relevant to individual contributors. I'd encourage both groups to read the book in it's entirety. Managers can always use a refresher on the challenges their teams face, and non-managerial staff may find it helpful to understand bigger picture issues and discover how they might support their managers in their efforts to further the goals of their teams.

CHAPTER 1

The Nuts and
Bolts that Hold
the In-House
Team Together

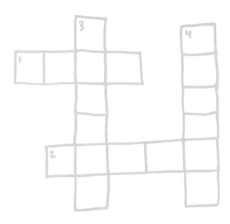

STAFFING STRATEGIES

Horizontal or vertical? Big or small? Specialists or general-
ists? These are the questions that most of you have to grapple
with every time you create a new budget, are hit with an ever-
increasing onslaught of projects or are asked to provide services you don't have the talent and skills for.

How you approach staffing your group should be determined by how creative you want your group to be, how much
you want to participate at a strategic level in your companies
and how varied you want your service offerings to be.

Of course, your company has a bit of a say in this proposition, too. You need to keep pace as they hopefully grow and
expand their products and services offerings, increase their
marketing efforts and enhance their brands. Their priorities
will ultimately determine how your team can best provide cost
savings and value to your clients. (Author's note: when using
the word *client* in this book, I am referring to your internal

corporate clients. You should be working with these internal clients in the same way an agency or studio would interact with their external clients.)

Key questions to consider include:

- Do you want to be a full-service agency?
- Are you okay with turning down work?
- Do you want to work on ground-up creative projects?
- Do you want to play a strategic role in your company?
- What are the needs of your company?
- What are the expectations of your company?
- Where are the places a creative team can make the biggest impact?

In the course of growing your team (should you be so lucky), beware of knee-jerk reactions to gaps in service. For example, when consistently confronted with an inability to meet deadlines because of workload, your initial response may be to hire another designer. Upon further reflection, though, it may make sense to hire a project manager and pull that function out from your designers. This would free them to take on more design projects, and you would end up with staff focused on their respective areas of expertise—design and project management.

> Getting a strong, strategically chosen team in place is only a fraction of the staffing equation.

Maintaining effective reporting structures, flexibility, morale, career development and performance must be your long-term goals. However, creatives are a varied, volatile lot who can be difficult to manage. It takes patience, insight and discipline to create and keep a team functioning at peak performance. Once you've gained the loyalty of this fickle group, though, you can count on them to pull together and support you and their peers with a passion, drive and commitment few teams in other departments can muster.

HOW TO HIRE

From business aptitudes to lifestyle and career goals, hiring in-house designers requires a focus on special skills, talents, attitudes and experience. It may take longer to find a designer who is a good corporate fit than if you were looking to fill an agency or design firm position. You may also need to use less traditional recruiting methods.

> Because of their unique structure and working environments, in-house groups require that their teams have skills above and beyond traditional design expertise.

Many more corporate creative teams have a flatter structure than their design firm and agency counterparts, necessitating that their designers be able to perform nondesign functions, such as project, vendor and client management. These responsibilities require excellent written and verbal communication skills and the abilities to prioritize, multitask and handle certain financial functions. Therefore, when hiring staff, you should be on the lookout for these skills, or at least for people with the potential to master them.

The challenge in securing talent with these additional business skills is that most designers don't receive this type of training in school, so, if you hire a recent grad, chances are you will need to invest time and money in schooling her in these areas. If you're in the market for more senior talent, you'll be more likely to find candidates whose prior in-house experience has provided them the opportunity to develop these needed business skills.

Be very careful when bringing agency talent into a corporate environment. Their expectations need to be realistically set regarding the environment, opportunities and logistical challenges they'll be facing as well as the increased need to rely on their business talents. It takes a special agency creative to thrive and grow in the in-house environment, but a good match can have a powerful and positive impact on your team.

I've found that networking is the best way to quickly locate good talent. Joining and participating in trade and industry organizations such as AIGA, HOW, DMI and InSource, among others, puts you in a position to meet large numbers of creatives

and gives them an opportunity to get to know you and your team as well.

> Sometimes, it's more effective to "bring the mountain to Mohammed."

An effective PR campaign that lands your team in the winning pages of various creative competitions, results in write-ups in various trade publications on successful in-house teams and affords presentation opportunities at various industry events will draw the talent you're looking for to you.

Many design schools, as well as industry groups, have graduate portfolio reviews, and many of these same institutions are putting more focus on design business skills. Locating and recruiting from them will give you a leg up on finding appropriate talent.

The more traditional methods of working with recruiters and posting on industry-specific job boards are also effective tools as long as you carefully communicate the skills and expertise you are looking for as well as what your company has to offer potential candidates.

To that point, it is absolutely essential that you create a detailed position description before you even begin your search and make sure to get approval on your description from upper management. Take care to set realistic expectations. Don't combine too many different skill sets in an attempt to work within a budget by filling multiple positions/functions with one head-count. You're not going to find a graphic designer who also has extensive web experience and can write copy and manage your traffic team, too.

In your position description, make sure you include:

- title
- reporting structure
- required design skills
- required business skills
- description of responsibilities
- prior experience requirements
- education requirements

Once you get candidates, your next responsibility is to carefully vet and interview them. As a creative, you're probably inclined to rely on your instincts and intuition, which have served you so well as a designer. While your gut is well suited to determine if a candidate's overall attitude and likeability is a good fit, it's not finely calibrated enough to determine specific interpersonal and business skills or the potential to adapt to your unique corporate work environment. This means you have to be a good detective and listen much more than you talk (a technique many interviewers neglect to put into practice).

Your questions should address issues such as collaboration, managing adversity, client management, project management and presentation skills. Even though I ragged on BMS' interview process in my prologue, there is valuable information that can be gleaned from answers to questions about how candidates handled work situations in their past engagements.

> Another important area to explore is whether the candidates' goals and expectations can be met working in your team.

Do they prize stability over peer recognition? Do they welcome the challenge of creating good design within strict limitations? Are they happy and willing to interact with clients on a daily basis?

I'd also recommend, if it isn't already baked into your interview process, that you have others (not those who would report into the potential candidates) interview them to gain other perspectives.

I know I'm stating the obvious but, as no candidate is perfect, you'll have to measure each one's strengths and weaknesses against your group's needs and priorities to gauge if he or she is a good fit.

A JACK-OF-ALL-TRADES OR A MASTER OF ONE: FLAT, AGENCY AND STUDIO MODELS

How your group's necessary functions are divided up among your team is one of the most important decisions you'll make. The type of work you do, the environment you work in and the needs and expectations of your clients should all be considered when choosing a model. If your projects are repetitive and logistically clear-cut, the flat structure may be appropriate. If, however, your jobs vary from one project to another, they are frequently revised and there is a lot of detail involved in their execution, the studio or agency model is probably a better choice. Below is a brief description of the three models to help guide you in your choice.

THE FLAT MODEL

This is the "jack-of-all-trades" model. Basically, your designers handle all functions associated with a project. These include the design of the assignment, of course, but also the project management, client contact, vendor management, proofreading and possibly billing responsibilities.

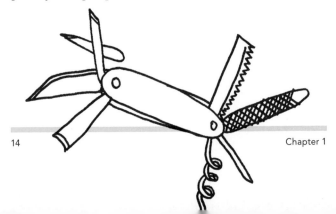

The description above is the extreme. There are variations. You may have a marketing team that handles some of these functions—especially the proofreading function. We designers are generally lousy proofreaders—we didn't become designers because we were good at spelling! But in essence, there are few, if any, nondesigners in the group in this model.

As previously mentioned, this model works best when the logistics of your projects remain the same, making the skills required for the nondesign functions easy to perform.

THE STUDIO MODEL

The studio model is similar to the flat model, with two key exceptions: a separate team handles the project management and administrative responsibilities, and another team handles production work. This leaves your designers with the design of the project as their primary focus. The more seasoned senior designers handle client contact. All of the logistics of the projects, such as job initiation, delivery of files to clients, coordination and documentation of client feedback, vendor management and billing are handled by project managers—staff with strengths in organizing, tracking and communicating information.

If your team handles projects that are logistically intensive, require review and approvals by multiple stakeholders, contain large amounts of detailed content, are on tight deadlines and require interfacing with a variety of outside vendors, this may be the best structure for your department.

THE AGENCY MODEL

The agency model has the most specialized structure of the three options discussed here. Most, if not all, of the departmental functions have specific positions designated to carry them out. There are production artists and designers. There are project managers and traffic staff. The agency model typically has individuals who buy print, acquire photography and illustrations, and research vendors who provide unique services for special projects.

A unique aspect of the agency model is that the creative team includes account executives who market and sell the group's services to the corporation at large and almost exclusively handle all client contact.

This model functions as an on-site agency that interfaces with and provides services for its clients in almost exactly the same way external agencies do. Departments based on this structure can only survive in large corporations that utilize a shared services model. Shared services is an arrangement where multiple companies or divisions under a larger corporate umbrella are required to go to an internal group to handle specific but common needs such as human resources, information technology or marketing services. In other words, the creative team's clients, who are working in the various corporate entities, are mandated to use the shared creative group to supply their creative and marketing deliverables instead of going to an outside vendor. Because these unique circumstances needed to justify the adoption of an agency model are rare, few in-house teams are structured that way.

MIX & MATCH: CONTRACT, FULL-TIMERS OR MAYBE BOTH

The use of contract workers, one of the biggest shifts in staffing to hit American businesses in recent years, made an early debut with in-house design teams. Formerly known in the design community as on-site freelancers, this group has steadily grown to a point where, now, many in-house teams employ this model—even at upper management levels.

While there are a number of advantages to partnering with contract workers, the magic number for positions to fill with this staff needs to be carefully considered. Too few and you risk overworking your designers and missing deadlines during periods of peak workload; too many and you risk having designers with hours of downtime. By establishing a flexible workforce that, at its largest, addresses your busiest times and, at its smallest, doesn't overwhelm your budget during slow periods, you'll be able to offer a truly effective cost-containment strategy to upper management.

Some points to consider when determining the right mix of full-time and contract workers include:

- Your need for internal institutional knowledge (having enough full-time staff who understand the unique marketing, regulatory and procedural requirements of your company)

- The amount of projects requiring specialized expertise (the number of one-off jobs that your full-time staff are not equipped to address)

- The variability of workload (how large are the swings in the amount of projects your team is asked to take on)

- The types of projects coming into your group (some of the more creative projects may be best handled by experienced hired guns under your direction who can collaborate and coach your full-time staff)

As the demands and variety of projects grow for in-house teams, so does the need for designers with specialized skills. Again, contract workers can support your team in meeting this challenge. If you bring in a web project but have only print designers on staff, rather than turn that project away, you can hire a web designer on a temporary basis.

Whether you work through staffing agencies or contact freelancers on your own, you should create a talent pool of outside designers with whom you can form strong bonds.

To accommodate the comings and goings of this transitory staff, you will have to set up pre-established workstations, e-mail accounts, network access and phone lines. An onboarding or new-hire training manual along with an assigned partner from your full-time staff will also help these designers hit the ground running when brought in to work on a project.

It's important to acknowledge and address the subtle prejudices and slights your contractors may encounter. Not being company employees, they may be barred from many company services and meetings including company gym access, company-wide town halls, training opportunities, holiday parties, etc. This understandably can damage morale and hinder your attempts to create a team culture between them and your full-timers. Whatever steps you can take to push the limits of these exclusionary policies and include your contract worker staff in company events will surely afford ample payback in enhanced morale and collaboration.

As with full-time hires, it's best to find staff who have had some experience working in a corporate environment. On the other hand, the agency culture and practices they bring could be beneficial to the team and may help get your group out of a creative rut if the agency talent is properly integrated into the department.

DIVIDE AND CONQUER

Divide and assign all departmental responsibilities to the people in your group who have the appropriate skills and expertise to best address those responsibilities and functions. For example, don't have a designer proofread (a practice that's reached epidemic proportions in the world of in-house). Designers are notoriously lousy spellers—no offense, but we didn't go into design because we love to spell and edit. By the same token, don't give production artists tier one design projects, web designers account management functions, or project coordinators print-buying responsibilities. I'm not implying that cross-functional training and growth shouldn't be pursued, but it's a good idea to play to people's current strengths and offer training opportunities for future growth and expanded responsibilities. Don't throw staff into a sink-or-swim situation. If you get pushback on requests for additional staff to fill gaps in certain areas, it might be a good idea to diplomatically point out that the finance team isn't called upon to create brochures nor is HR requested to create posters or annual reports. Why then should a designer be asked to do account and project management? It's not efficient, it leads to costly mistakes and it impacts morale and job satisfaction. It's an advantage for an in-house team to be as flat as possible, but the group will hit a point of diminishing returns if this tactic is taken too far.

A sobering aside: In a 2008 AIGA in-house survey, a large majority of the respondents noted that they spent almost half of their workday on nondesign related activities. This is probably not the best use of their time and skills and can lead to costly attrition. Agencies figured this out long ago. They have an account management team for client interface, traffic teams for project coordination, bookkeepers for financial functions and administrators for the day-to-day handling of logistics. The same efficiencies apply to corporate creative departments. If you can't get funding for additional staff to handle non-design functions, you may be able to leverage staff in other groups. Be sure that whoever is doing these tasks has some understanding of the unique issues surrounding the creative process.

WALK A MILE IN THEIR SHOES

While taking all of the above into account, it is still very helpful, on a number of levels, to cross-train in-house teams. Most obviously, members of your team will be better able to pitch in when work floods specific areas within the team or when staff is absent. There's the added benefit of different members of the

team gaining an appreciation and respect for the other groups within their department. For teams that hand off projects to other teams, there is the possibility that staff will be more considerate in how and what they hand off to the others. You can even apply this practice to your clients. Having a designer shadow a client not only allows for a greater appreciation on the part of the designer of the challenges that clients face, but also helps enhance the relationship.

STRIKE A BALANCE

At the end of the day (as they say in the corporate world) though, it's important to strike a balance between expanding each of your staff's areas of expertise and focusing on their strengths. Fear of taking on new challenges should never determine how far you and your team reach beyond the skills and positions you're currently comfortable with, yet everyone has innate strengths and passions they should play to, and to deny these is counterproductive and damaging to morale.

I remember working with a particularly talented designer whom I wanted to push to the next level. In my mind, moving

up meant more client contact. The individual's design talents, though, didn't translate into customer service and client interface skills. The project was a disaster, and it took me months to repair the damaged relationship with the client. I would have been better off not imposing my independent opinion on how the designer should have grown. If we had discussed what he perceived to be his interests and strengths, we could have determined other areas, such as interactive design or branding development, as better pursuits.

Conversely, to continually default to strengths because of a consistent knee-jerk reaction to immediate needs is a short-term approach that will expose your group to risk of inflexibility and damage the professional confidence of your creatives.

ADVISE BUT DON'T CONSENT

Designers should not take on functions they are not trained to handle, but they should be willing to step in and help when other departments need assistance with making decisions that are related to design. There are plenty of tasks associated with the creation of marketing materials and the management of a creative team that designers can assist in by giving advice. For example, even if the purchasing department is in charge of print procurement as part of their overall responsibilities, they may not have enough knowledge of printing to effectively manage print projects. As a designer, you're in a unique position to clarify printing issues that will aid the purchasing specialist in making informed decisions. The same idea holds true for HR. Their grasp of the specific skill sets and experience that designers need to have may be limited by their lack of experience with the practice of design. Design managers are in the best position to assist HR staff in developing performance metrics and interview priorities specific to designers. In fact, in this instance, it's in your best interest to be involved. This ensures that you're being evaluated for your true contributions, skills and strengths, not some arbitrary standardized list of evaluation points that have nothing to do with your job.

By helping members in other departments, you establish yourself as a strategic expert, strengthen your relationships with your peers in other groups and exert some control over areas that either affect the outcome of a project or the management of your team.

None of the staffing strategies I'm speaking about here are rocket science, but in the frequently overwhelming world of

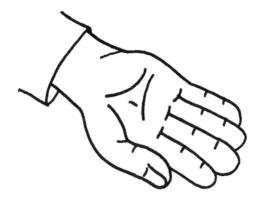

corporate design, practicing these strategies often gets thrown to the wayside.

> The key is to build in opportunities to assess where you and your team are in regard to mandated responsibilities and professional fulfillment on a consistent basis and in an honest manner.

Then you need to act on those assessments. If you have a formalized quarterly review process mandated by HR, try to build this additional assessment into that process. If not, create quarterly or biannual professional reviews. On a group-wide scale, hold meetings as a team to discuss where you are in terms of services and functions. Identify any disconnects and decide how best to address them. If you're not proactive, you'll be at the mercy of inefficient processes defined by bad habits and, worse, have your staffing and HR strategies be determined by other departments that don't understand the design process and will impose irrelevant or counterproductive staffing mandates on your team.

THE BUDDY SYSTEM: HOW NOT TO LOSE YOUR WAY

There's a reason departments are often referred to as teams. Their success lies in your ability and your team's ability to work together and support each other and your clients by filling in each other's skill-set gaps, coverage gaps and knowledge gaps.

Right off the bat, I'd recommend pairing designers into teams of two. There can be a primary and secondary designer on a particular project, but by buddying up, you can be assured that you'll have coverage, quality control checks and brand and client knowledge covered in a way that the one designer per project model can never assume.

KNOW WHAT YOU KNOW

Imagine flying in an airplane and suddenly finding out that the captain passed out and there was no co-pilot. A pretty unnerving thought, huh? Now try imagining your team leader, pre-press expert or project coordinator of ten years suddenly taking a new job with no backup, assistant or documented guide of how he works or whom he works with. While this may not be life threatening like the first scenario, it could still cause a lot of angst and hand wringing. Institutional, operational and brand knowledge are the biggest assets your team possesses after its design and creative skills. They're also the primary differentiators between your team and outside design firms and agencies, and are critical to your long-term business health and success, so you better protect those assets through knowledge documentation, knowledge transfer and a viable, well-maintained succession plan.

Every member of your team should have a trained backup. All of your key team members need to create a file that documents their responsibilities, work procedures and key contacts. Every project should have a team assigned to it at its inception. Only then can you be sure that you will be able to provide high-quality, value-added and consistently good service for your company.

CONTINUING EDUCATION

When designers start their careers, it quickly becomes obvious that additional training is required in order for them to be successful as individual designers and as productive members of their team. This is especially true for in-house designers who function in an environment that demands skills and behaviors that don't come naturally to creatives—and that are often not addressed in design school.

Almost all designers, within their first week of their first job after graduation, are walloped with the realization that there are a whole lot of things they weren't taught in design school. That is especially true for designers working in-house where there's a never-ending maze of policies, procedures and politics to navigate in addition to practicing design. Some of the lessons designers need to learn, they're going to learn the hard way— by making mistakes and, ideally, learning from those mistakes. Fortunately, there are other ways available. If you're the newbie, honestly assess where you need the most support and put some of the suggestions below into action.

One of the most powerful ways to learn the ropes of in-house design is to find mentors and develop relationships with them. Not only can they teach you how to succeed in the corporate environment, but they can become advocates for you as well. Some mentors will be working in your company, others you may be aware of through personal avenues and professional affiliations. Different mentors will have different areas of expertise. I remember having a difficult time understanding and negotiating the intimidating realm of corporate politics. I worked with a man who was brilliant at it. Through my relationship with him, I gradually came to understand that corporate politics were not to be feared or loathed but used as a tool to forward my goals and the goals of my team. It wasn't just helpful facts that I acquired, but a whole new mindset.

You should also pay attention to co-workers who exhibit behaviors and styles you believe are counterproductive to your success. You'll see in excruciating detail what not to do and possibly how others successfully deal with those individuals. I once worked with a manager who was self-absorbed and more concerned with impressing upper management and moving up the corporate ladder than in supporting her team. I learned much by watching how her second-in-command managed his relationship with her and succeeded in spite of her misplaced priorities.

Being a mentor can also be an educational experience. Mentoring puts you in a position where you have to actively consider the issues you're advising on and then effectively communicate your views. When you're exposed to the challenges of the professional you're supporting, you are forced to define and clarify your response. This prepares you to address similar challenges you may one day end up having to confront.

More formal paths available to many in-house designers include management and business skills training programs that most companies offer their employees. Contact your HR department, check the courses out and try not to prejudge them. Expert consultants, who effectively address important in-house competencies that were never even mentioned in design school, run many of these programs.

If you equate self-awareness with education, you should see if your HR department will conduct a 360-degree global review for you. This is an eye opening exercise in which your peers, reports and managers are asked to rate you (anonymously) on a series of criteria and metrics relevant to your business acumen including your leadership, collaborative, problem-solving and communication aptitudes. It's a great tool to see yourself as others do and target opportunities to improve the way you conduct yourself in the business environment.

Outside of the corporate realm, there are more traditional opportunities to further your education and fill in gaps around business skills. The most obvious are adult education classes offered by most colleges and universities. In addition, there are also two- or three-day workshops sponsored by design industry organizations that also afford you the opportunity to meet peers from other companies. Industry conferences are another great resource for quickly honing your design and design business skills. Many conferences now have in-house seminar tracks specifically designed to address the challenges you face in your job.

> Giving presentations to your peers in the design community is an unusual but effective way to expand your design and design management skills and knowledge.

Obviously, it's good training for presenting to groups of people—a pretty common function of being an in-house designer. In addition, preparing for a presentation is like writing a term paper. You have to define your topic, research it and then analyze and synthesize the information you've gathered into a coherent outline. Picking a subject for a seminar about which you wish to learn or explore more opens up the opportunity to delve into it in a way that you might otherwise not have. Of course, there's the additional value of enhancing your reputation within the design community possibly leading to more professional opportunities.

An even more intense way to continue your education is to teach. To be successful at teaching, you have to immerse yourself in the subject your course is about. It's also important that you generate dialogue during your classes with your students. From those discussions, you will learn from the students enrolled in your course—either through their questioning or the unique insights they offer. Teaching is personally rewarding, too. It can be gratifying to support and nurture young designers, and it is inspiring to be in the presence of their passion and unbounded optimism about the power of design and their ability to contribute to it.

If teaching is not workable for you, participating in portfolio reviews is a lesser commitment that still brings you in touch with young designers and their enthusiasm. These reviews force you to assess your views and priorities about design and then articulate those views to help guide those whom you're supporting.

Judging awards competitions is a great way to stretch your analytical skills and learn more about the subtleties of design and the design business landscape. It forces you to consider the aesthetics and business principles behind the work you're reviewing, and seeing how others approach design problems expands your repertoire of design solutions. Interacting with the other judges provides additional opportunities to expand your views about design.

THE MORAL OF MORALE

In the midst of major corporate breakdowns, downsizing or other difficult challenges, upper management's patent response is often, "Hey, let's throw a party! That'll cheer up the troops!" Don't fiddle while Rome burns. I've witnessed this absurdly inappropriate response to poor morale over and over again. And no matter if it's a buddy-up breakfast, a team-building lunch or an appreciation dinner, they all have the same effect on morale—zippo, nada, none, or morale dips even lower.

There are a number of other reactions to poor morale that have equally ill effects. A small bonus, a day off, a nice note left on the desk or a "thank you for all you've done" e-mail only makes the giver look out of touch, inept or callous if your team is dealing with large or chronic issues that are challenging them in unsustainable ways. After the tenth eighty-hour week with no overtime or end in sight, a fifteen dollar gift certificate to iTunes is just going to make someone angry.

So what to do? First, level with your team about the challenges and acknowledge the burden they're bearing without the

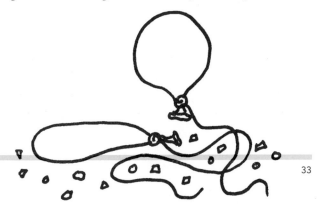

corporate spin. They're not ten-year-olds, so don't talk to them that way. This doesn't mean you have license to trash upper management or bad-mouth the company—a trap many managers fall into—which only gives your team permission to do the same and behave like a group of victims or, worse, gives them an excuse to underperform to get even with "the man." Just be honest and be human.

The next thing you need to do is address the issues impacting your team to the best of your ability. That probably means having assertive conversations with the appropriate co-workers in the departments in the best position to address the problems you and your team are facing. If it's an infrastructure issue, such as the need for better equipment, office space, networking capabilities, etc., then push for the additional resources. If it's a workload issue, explore ways to get more staff, sub it out or reduce the load by weeding out unnecessary projects.

Of course, you always need to make an ironclad case for your requests, so be prepared with plenty of backup and make sure to always keep the communications factual and unemotional in tone. (See "The Buying Conversation: Get What You Need" in chapter five.)

> Let your team know of your efforts and keep them updated on your progress. Sometimes the mere act of fighting for your team mitigates much of the bad feelings they might have about the situation.

When things are going well from a macro perspective, you should focus your morale-building efforts on enhancing your team's working environment. This is not a one-size-fits-all proposition. Each member of the group has unique goals and desires. Discussing their personal goals and looking for ways to support them in achieving their goals will have a much deeper and long-lasting impact on their morale than an extra day off.

I'm not advocating ignoring the little pleasures in (work) life. There is always a place for heartfelt and frequent thank yous, bowling parties, gift certificates, inspiration days, off-site lunches, free bottled water, etc. It's just that these acts will only have a positive impact once the more fundamental issues of professional and personal fulfillment are addressed.

CREATIVE OUTERSPACE, CREATIVE INNERSPACE

Quality of life and a workplace that is personally and professionally fulfilling is now often a higher priority than pay for designers. Unfortunately, there are a number of factors—some historical, others relatively new—which challenge an in-house team's desired physical and psychological workspace. And while there are ways to impact and improve these environments, it's also important to understand that creatives need to adjust their expectations and mindset as to what their workplace has to offer.

The three basic problem areas that almost every corporate creative team must grapple with include high turnover, a poor physical workspace and a restrictive client and corporate culture.

Companies today have a revolving door when it comes to staff. Between co-workers working remotely, the use of consultants and contract workers, and the volatility of permanent employees' tenure, the person sitting in the cube next to you could be different on any given day. As a team member, you have a responsibility to contribute to your group's need for community in spite of these challenges. As an individual designer working in a team in constant flux, there are ways to create a secure sense of place that will enable you to do your best work.

First and foremost, it's important to make a good first impression. Often, once new team members are chosen to come on board, getting them the tools and access they need to do their job is pushed off to the last minute, sometimes even to the day they start. Aside from not making the best use of their first days or weeks in the group and costing your company money, this creates an impression with the new hires that either your team isn't buttoned up or, worse, that you and your team really don't value them. Make sure that, as much as your corporate bureaucracy will allow, e-mail access, ID badges, network access, phone, computer and office space are all in place the day your new hires arrive. Assign them an "onboarding buddy" to show them the ropes. Introduce them to the entire team in a live meeting, not an e-mail announcement. Encourage your team to stop by and personally say hello.

For staff who are on the other side of the working continuum and are about to leave, the way their departure is handled impacts not only them but the team that remains. It's important to respectfully and professionally treat staff members who are moving on, no matter the circumstances of their leaving. The other members of the group closely watch and form their opinion of the department based on how well or poorly departures are orchestrated. The team members leaving are also going to represent your group to others in the industry. This makes

them important contributors to your future recruiting efforts. If they are leaving on good terms, a going-away party may be appropriate. Conducting an exit interview is a great tool to get candid feedback that may lead to ideas and actions to improve your team and gives the departing employees a sense that you value them and their opinions.

Staff who are witnessing the movement of creatives into and out of their group need to feel valued and respected and that they have some control over their environment. They need to be involved in strategic and tactical initiatives, such as workflow processes, archiving procedures, departmental goals and roles, and responsibilities decisions. They also need to be informed, as early as possible, of any changes that will impact the group and why those decisions were made. More than recognizing life events like birthdays, marriages and new children, day-to-day conversations about their personal lives, interests and personal and career goals will communicate to them that they aren't just a number on a spreadsheet or a corporate cog.

> Most importantly, honest, accurate communication devoid of corporate-speak and euphemisms will let them know they're being dealt with respectfully and professionally.

Companies are always out to maximize efficiencies, and when it comes to physical space, that mandate translates into the ubiquitous cubicle, a.k.a. "the cube." Nothing hinders communication, personal space and self-expression more effectively than "the cube." The creative process is collaborative; "the cube" is not.

At the very least, make sure your teams are in cube clusters and that they have common areas for impromptu meetings. As much as the corporate bureaucracy will permit, allow your creatives to personalize their cubes with custom lighting, posters, collections, plants, etc.

The place where your team spends most of its time—the cyberworld—should be open to self-expression. Individualized desktops, icons and alerts should be encouraged as long as they don't impede necessary archiving and equipment-sharing needs. If in compliance, even certain widgets and custom applications should be permitted.

In order to give in-house creatives some control over their aural space, MP3 players should be allowed. Not only do these devices set creative moods for the team, they also block out distracting background chatter that can slow down the creative process.

In-house groups often feel as if they exist outside of the company culture. This is inevitable given the fact that the creative team has a different mandate, working process and culture from their counterparts in other departments. It's best to strike a balance between adopting the rah-rah corporate mindset and maintaining the "rebel with a cause" cowboy attitude. There are advantages to both in enhancing and maintaining a positive working environment.

All human beings want to feel that they're contributing to something, be it to a company, a cause or another individual. It's imperative that a clear line be drawn that connects your team's responsibilities to the company's goals in the most altruistic way possible. Having presentations—by heads of departments responsible for R&D, customer relations and sales—that give your team a deeper and broader perspective on your company and how they contribute to its mission can help establish this connection. Distributing letters from satisfied customers and clients can also make your team's efforts take on a more personal dimension.

The other side of the creative's psyche, though, involves being a rebel, an individual and a nonconformist—hardly the makings of a good corporate citizen. If you try to toe the company line on teamwork and compliance without a wink and a nod to the absurdity of some of those mandates, you'll lose the

Chapter 1

respect and commitment of your team. It's a tightrope to be sure, but there are ways to walk it.

Poking good-natured fun at the company bureaucracy is a great way to diffuse frustration and anger. I remember receiving a three-page memo from facilities on how to properly use the newly installed turnstiles, which pretty much required just putting your card on the reader and walking through. Our team wrote up mock instructions on how to open a door, flush a toilet, etc. Mocking the proliferation of corporate acronyms is another harmless but effective exercise in venting. Groups that I worked with would create lists of ridiculous and amusing takes on existing and concocted acronyms. There are many easy targets in a corporation to satirize, just make sure that the satire doesn't turn hateful, personal or malicious.

Slightly subversive expressions of creative solidarity can help make working in a corporate setting more palatable. Have a "designer black" dress day. Create buttons with slogans like "Designers Do It." At one company where I worked, we used the Homeland Security alert legend for project priorities.

In addition to changing your and your team's environment, some inner recalibration can help your morale as well. A dose of realistic expectations on your part is required to maintain a healthy attitude towards your work environment. Don't expect your job to satisfy your creative muse—look elsewhere to scratch that itch. Don't expect your job to meet your need for friendship, though you should experience a sense of camaraderie with your peers. And don't look to your career to fulfill your need of leading a purposeful life, though there are opportunities to be giving and supportive of others.

Do expect respect, fair play, support and compensation for your talent, hard work and experience. If you can get that, the rest will fall into place, and your company will become a place you enjoy going to both on a professional and personal level. In-house is not a home, but given that you spend a large part of your life there, it better be pretty close.

Of all the debilitating and demoralizing situations foisted upon in-house groups by their parent companies, lack of resources and accompanying unrealistic expectations are the worst. Corporate creative teams are often understaffed, underequipped and underfunded. They are given less time to complete projects than their peers in outside agencies and are paid less money. Under these circumstances, resignation and apathy begin to eat away at the cultural fabric of the team.

Unfortunately, while these issues are the most destructive to the department, they are also the most difficult to address. To be perfectly candid, there are three options. Convince your managers and their managers of your team's value and secure more funding. Get your group moved under a manager who has a greater appreciation for your department. Or quit and find a company that values and supports in-house creative teams.

INFRASTRUCTURE: THE HOUSE THAT JACK BUILT

Infrastructure is not just about the tangible—your digital network, office furniture, cubes and monitors. It's also about the intangible: your culture, emotional space and relationships. It's critical to acknowledge that the tangible and intangible are intertwined.

In *The Tipping Point*, Malcolm Gladwell speaks to the impact that people's physical environment can have on their beliefs and, consequently, their behaviors. Gladwell refers to a theory called "The Broken Windows" that was developed to explain the rise of crime in certain New York neighborhoods. The theory asserts that the appearance of a broken window

that goes unrepaired over time leads the neighborhood residents to assume that no one cares about that area. They begin to believe that because of this apathy they can commit offenses without consequences. The broken window also impacts their sense of self-worth: No one cares enough about them and their neighborhood to improve it. The residents start to act out. More windows are broken, only reinforcing and validating their original beliefs. Pretty soon, in addition to the broken windows, people start throwing garbage on the sidewalks, urinating in the street and hustling passersby.

Much evidence has been gathered to support this theory, and I contend that it applies to business organizations as well, and especially creative teams who are unusually tuned in to their environments. Therefore, you should take care to notice and address the seemingly small and subtle but incessant indignities that your team may be enduring, whether in their physical or psychological space. If there is a particularly abusive client, move quickly to manage them. If your team is complaining about the harsh office lighting, purchase better light bulbs and homier lighting fixtures. If they keep encountering needed graphics websites being censored by IT's security program, work with IT to get those sites exempted.

As miniscule and nitpicky as these issues may appear, when suffered in aggregate or constantly over time, they can deeply affect your team's culture and effectiveness.

RUBBERBANDWIDTH

There probably isn't an in-house team that hasn't at one time or another had to deal with inadequate network infrastructure. Graphics files are bigger than most business files typically stored in a company's computer network. If you're in a Mac studio, you'll face cross-platform issues with your PC-based counterparts. To compound the problem, IT staffers seem to take complaints about this problem as a personal affront, becoming defensive and oppositional.

The best way to deal with these issues is to expose the impact they have on your team's efficiency and make the case for special accommodations. For file transfers with remote locations, the establishment of a secure FTP site may be in order. If IT is unable to meet your needs, there are always third-party providers you can turn to. I've always been amazed at how cooperative IT groups become when faced with outsourced solutions.

ROLL OUT THE RED CARPET: RESOURCES FOR NEW STAFF

I remember being flabbergasted when I started at a new job in a large and, I mistakenly assumed, efficient corporation. I discovered on my first day that I did not have a phone, computer, e-mail, corporate ID, network access, paper, pens, pencils, stapler, tape, calendar or even a chair. I did have an office, though I quickly had to give that up when the painters arrived. It took much longer to get those other services than it took for the walls to dry.

> Not being able to get your company to provide even the most basic tools needed by your team to do their jobs is very costly.

It results in frustration, bad first impressions, lost productivity and general confusion. Customer service is a concept that many of the departments that support you don't seem to grasp.

Unfortunately, it becomes the team's job to move the monolithic bureaucracy along. It takes an individual skilled in the arts of cajoling, manipulating, threatening, bribing and tact to successfully get even the simplest of needs filled. If that's not you, then find the right person and do whatever it takes to keep him happy and part of your team.

In the absence of that talented individual, here are some tips to goose things along.

- Make nice with those who can help. Take the IT guy out to lunch. Invite the facilities director to your team's holiday party. Bring your HR representative into your departmental strategic meetings. Make these individuals feel like they have a personal connection to your team.

- Plan ahead and reserve your place in line for needed services. If you anticipate pulling in five contractors at a clip for an upcoming crunch, contact facilities and give them the heads-up. Better yet, at budget time, request that workstations and cubes be outfitted and ready to roll well in advance of incoming temps.

- Never voice your frustration to those that refuse to support you. Clearly state your needs and slowly move up the chain of command when you don't get traction, but be open and transparent with those whom you're leapfrogging.

- Always speak to the business rationale behind your requests. Also note the lost efficiencies if you don't get the help you've requested.

In the event that you can't get what you need, which you probably won't, create workarounds. Use web e-mail accounts as a stopgap. Utilize cell phones, lease temporary computers, borrow furniture from conference rooms. Always remember that it's easier to ask for forgiveness than permission.

KEEP YOUR IN-HOUSE IN ORDER: ASSET MANAGEMENT

IT'S THE DAM, DAMNIT!

Digital asset management, or DAM, is one of the most neglected opportunities available to your in-house team to increase your efficiencies (read "more time for the fun stuff") and the value that you offer your company (read "cost savings"). If you already have a software solution, you can pat yourself on the back, but know that having your files stored in a digital warehouse is only one part of the process needed for archiving and managing creative files, plans, documents and printed materials.

How many times have you or your team spent more hours on finding legacy images, layouts and logos needed for a par-

ticular project than on that project's actual design. It may be costly, time-consuming and painful to adopt a DAM solution, but your efforts will be rewarded almost immediately upon implementing a digital asset storage system and database.

A note of caution: Don't let your time restrictions, budget or personal resistance to the process determine the kind of DAM solution you decide on. The choice should only be dictated by your need—which, of course, means you have to do some kind of needs assessment up front (what fun!).

POSSESSION IS NINE-TENTHS OF THE BATTLE

Do you possess the files that have been created for your clients by external agencies? If your team repurposes existing design for new uses, then you'd better start to partner with the outside firms and get the goods. Having those files upfront and not having to scramble and negotiate before you can even take a stab at creating layouts for those rush projects that require another group's files will come in handy.

Agencies may be loath to release their designs to you, and you may want to protect your relationships with them. Have your procurement or purchasing department work through this process instead of you having to beg and threaten to get what you need. If this doesn't work, you can always approach the vendors who printed or hosted the work and get the files from them. This approach also ensures that, should the vendor have made any changes subsequent to a handoff from an agency, you'll have the most up-to-date files.

TAKE STOCK OF YOUR STOCK ART

If you purchase rights managed or royalty images, you'd better track the usage guidelines and make sure that you don't recycle an old image you no longer own the rights to or use it in media that you haven't paid for.

I remember creating an entire website focused on my company's product line without first negotiating web usage of the photos. Let's just say our team's relationship with the photographer went south and our competency was called into question by upper management.

And don't expect your marketing teams to have this handled or to understand the intricacies or rationale of usage agreements. Many of them actually believe they can go online and copy and paste into their marketing materials any photo they find on a website without paying for it. Given this lack of understanding, there is no way they're in a position to handle the stock art usage issues. Act as their consultant and reinforce your value to them while saving your company from litigation and fines.

METADATA MEGACARE

Just because you dumped all of your assets willy-nilly into the mouth of your DAM software solution doesn't mean you'll be able to find them at the push of a button. The system will only work as well as you manage it. This means that you need to assign metadata or content tags to your assets that define what the files are. The more data or descriptors you assign to a file, the more ways that become available for you to locate it.

You or another designer may only remember the name of the project, or the project number or the approximate date it was created. A client may ask for a legacy file by the publication name that it appeared in or the customer it was developed for. Having more tags greatly increases the speed and ease with which you can navigate the hundreds or thousands of files you've archived.

Logistically, this means that someone actually has to devote a fair amount of time working with the software to tag the assets. You may want to have the creator of the file assign the descriptors or hire a staffer to take this function on full time. The circumstances of your business, number of projects, budget, and number of tags you want to assign should determine your approach. One thing's for sure, without taking this on, you'll be destined to spend more time than you can imagine searching through folders and opening files when you could have been designing.

ARCHIVING: CONNECT WITH YOUR INNER LIBRARIAN

You and your team may juggle dozens of projects a day. If your group is large and the projects complex, a single file could be touched by multiple designers making multiple revisions to multiple versions of a project in a matter of hours. Under these circumstances, how you label and store your files can make all the difference between success on a project and a complete crash and burn.

I've witnessed (too many times to count) files being lost, multiple versions of a design being live at the same time, and

outdated files being sent to clients—and worse, being handed off to printers. The kinds and number of calamities that can occur without disciplined, well thought-out file-naming conventions should be enough to scare any in-house design team into adopting them.

The number of variables and the variety of unique business needs different in-house groups have make it impossible to give very specific advice, but a general list of file specific information to document in the filename include:

- business unit
- brand
- outside customer
- client (department)
- project date
- stage of project (concept, layout, final mechanical)
- version
- type of media (brochure, poster, display)
- purpose (educational, sales aid, internal presentation)

PROCESSING THE PROCESS PROCESS: STANDARD OPERATING PROCEDURES

This mind-bending title was purposely chosen to showcase the kind of confusion most creatives experience when confronted with having to create, implement or follow directions, procedures, SOPs or policies—pretty much everything involved with working in a corporate environment. Designers who are required to follow process either freeze like a deer in the headlights or rebel against the corporate machine and attempt to stick it to "the man" by ignoring the rules and doing things their way.

If you're a creative team manager, you're now "the man," and if you're not, you're working for the man on his turf, in his game, and you need to play by his rules. And by the way, these rules can actually get you to a place where you can spend more of your time doing what you really love—design.

PPPPPP

Commit this to memory: Proper Process Prevents Piss-Poor Performance.

All creative groups, no matter what company they're in, how large or small they are, and regardless of the services they offer, need SOPs (standard operating procedures). The primary purpose of process and procedures is to standardize, document and, most importantly, dictate the flow of work moving through their creative departments. Other benefits include ensuring that there are effective means of communication between their department and their clients, peers and other departments in the organizations, that quality controls are in place, that their staff understands expectations and can be held accountable to those expectations, and that new hires can walk into their groups and quickly get down to the work of designing great creative pieces for their companies. Now take a breath; it gets harder.

Everyone on the team involved in the creative and production process may know his specific role and his stage of the workflow, but that's not good enough. You can't all read each other's thoughts when trying to grasp the entire creative process and neither can your clients, upper management or new hires. It would also be a very bad idea to rely on the accuracy of their or your memory. Therefore, your SOPs need to be carefully and clearly created and documented. If your group is large (ten-plus people), or you have a variety of complex project types, you may want to bring in an outside consultant for this phase.

Documenting your processes and procedures is a painful process that can frequently fall by the wayside in the face of time-sensitive projects, but you need to acknowledge your SOP's importance and be disciplined in completing it. The conundrum is confounding: You can't complete your SOPs because you're constantly faced with putting out fires, but the fires won't ever go away until you implement rigorous SOPs. You really need to acknowledge that many of the fires you face every day are a result of a lack of process or a lack of alignment from your team, your clients and your company around existing process. If you don't believe in the positive power of process, just ask yourself how many times you've had to redo a project because there wasn't a creative brief, how many times files have been lost or overwritten due to sloppy archiving practices, and how many times the lack of quality control has resulted in frustrated clients at best or reprinted jobs at worst.

THE PLAN PLAN

So it's time to do the work. Simply put:

1. Write down the process as you believe it to be.
2. Meet with your team to refine it.
3. Review it with your clients and other departments that your group works with to confirm accuracy and validity.
4. Refine it based on feedback.
5. Get final buy-in from key stakeholders and staff.

Your final deliverable should be a flowchart that details the life cycle of a project. After all that work, you're only a third of the way there. Lucky you.

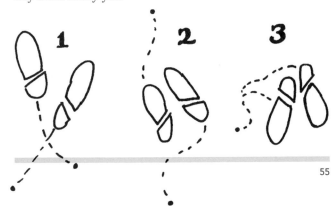

YOU'RE ON THE DETAIL DETAIL

Your flowchart, recorded in chronological order, is a compilation of steps required to complete a project. Every step in your process has tasks associated with it. The tasks often involve multiple staff. You need to create the work instructions for each staff member associated with a particular step. If the step is a project kickoff, you may have an account person involved who needs to set up a kickoff meeting, a designer who needs to create a preliminary brief, a print buyer who needs to initiate a spec sheet. The work instructions are a drill-down from the broader, more high-level workflow flowchart.

> A key point here is that there may be policies associated with tasks.

A policy is a rule that must be followed, which is distinct from a task, which is a function that should be performed. An example of a policy that is associated with a task would be: All assignments given to outside photographers must have a PO cut before the assignment begins. This is very different from the task description, which would be: The art director creates a PO upon initiating an assignment with an outside photographer. Policies must be followed; tasks are more fluid and subject to judgment calls if there is no accompanying policy.

The final deliverable for work instructions is generally a chart that lists the participants in each particular step and describes the tasks they need to perform at that step.

AN EMBRACE IS NOT A HUG

You now have your workflow diagram and the associated tasks or work instructions. Now comes the hardest part—as if getting to this point wasn't painful enough. You need to work with your team, other departments and your clients to ensure adoption of your group's SOPs. Training and education, of course, come first. You can hold seminars, create hardcopy training materials or web-based educational modules. Certification through testing to ensure understanding of the SOPs is also a good idea.

Most important, though, is to create a mindset in which your team and your clients recognize the value of the SOPs and their adherence to them. It's pretty much a carrot and stick affair. The carrot? For the designers, it's the promise of smoother workflows with less time spent tracking down lost

files and deciphering unclear communications. This results in fewer rounds of revisions and more time to do what they love, which is, of course, design. For copywriters, it's clearer expectations, initial direction and subsequent feedback, allowing them to quickly hone in on the appropriate tone and content. For the client, it's cleaner, better, quicker service and deliverables. On the stick side, it's poor performance reviews and low merit increases for your team if they don't adopt the SOPs and substandard work for the clients. If you have a formal HR staff review process in place, you can set goals and objectives for you team around the adoption of your SOPs. If you do your job right, your team and clients will embrace the SOPs. But be patient; it will take time. It's important to note that you'll need to reinforce adoption of the SOPs even after initial training and buy-in. It's easier for people to ignore rigorous process than to follow it.

WITH PAIN THERE'S GAIN

Obviously, putting SOPs into place won't happen overnight, and it will be challenging and downright painful most of the time. Once you've successfully implemented your SOPs, though, you'll find yourself and your team functioning in an exceptional work environment with more time to do what everyone loves and with more successful projects and happy clients than you ever could have imagined. As they say in corporatese: a pretty good return on investment by anybody's standards.

AN ARMY OF ONE

Many in-house departments are made up of a sole designer who often reports to the marketing or sales department. Obviously, if you're one of these multi-talented individuals, you are most likely called upon to perform a variety of functions for your company, including but not limited to: art direction, graphic design, web design, vendor management, procurement, computer maintenance, copywriting, proofreading, photography, project management, client management, brand consultant, trade show booth design, digital printer … I'm running out of breath here, and you probably get the picture (and should be patting yourself on your overburdened back).

While many of the topics already covered may be a bit broad for your situation, most are completely appropriate, scalable and applicable. Defining and documenting process, establishing healthy client relationships and practicing good operational and business hygiene are certainly just as appropriate and useful to a department of one as to a team of one hundred. But there are challenges and opportunities unique to single designer creative departments.

SPREAD THE WEALTH

Management of workload tops the list. Chances are, day in and day out, you are called on to complete an unmanageable amount of work. You are likely a department of one because your company doesn't want to spend a lot of money on design. They're either cheap or they don't understand and appreciate the value that good design brings to their marketing and sales efforts. Whatever the reason, your best approach for expanding your staff is to present the option of hiring on-site contract workers.

There are several reasons why you may meet with success in better management of your workload by adopting this strategy.

First, and most important to your upper management, you only spend money when you have to.

As workload increases, you bring in outside resources; when it diminishes, you scale back. You can also bring in talent suited to specific projects. If you're updating your website, you bring in a freelancer with expertise in web design. If it's a trade show booth, you do the same in choosing talent for that project. There are no benefits expenses to be born by your company, and you don't have to deal with any of the HR monitoring and interference that comes with full-time headcount.

Having your freelancers work on-site allows you greater creative control, affords your clients access to the talent for better, unfiltered marketing direction, and lets your manager see for herself that the work is getting done. Of course, you will also need on-site resources to support your freelancers, so there's a better chance you can get that additional workstation, color printer and enhanced Internet pipeline you've been pining for.

A slightly Machiavellian motive for bringing in contract workers on-site is that it allows your upper management to get used to, even dependent on, having additional creative staff. It's not uncommon for on-site freelancers to convert to full-time headcount. In other words, it's a backdoor tactic for getting the larger full-time staff you know would best benefit you and your company.

"OH, REVERED ONE"

Most in-house creative teams are constantly struggling with gaining the respect they deserve and require to best perform their job. This challenge is especially difficult, and critical, for a team of one.

Many strategies for achieving respect are covered in other sections of this book, but there are a few that are especially effective for single-person creative departments.

> One of the most powerful actions you can take is to consistently forge strong personal relationships with your clients and upper management.

As the sole representative of your department, you're in the enviable position of being able to communicate a focused message about your competencies, achievements and the value you bring to the company. Constantly reaching out to key stakeholders in your company by having lunches, formal and informal face-to-face meetings and written communications will establish your credibility and build trust, resulting in the respect you need to service your company.

A formal capabilities presentation that catalogues all the services you provide and documents the cost savings to the company may not be the first thing you would think to do as a department of one, but it is well worth considering. Chances are your clients and managers have no idea of the depth and breadth of the services you provide. Presenting your capabilities in a formal, well thought-out and designed presentation showcases your professionalism and commitment to your job.

As the lone in-house creative, you probably have to deal with the Chinese takeout syndrome, where you're looked upon as an order taker and short order cook with little or no opportunity to provide input on strategy or even to suggest the best methods for a project's implementation. You're often told to "just get it done" whether the "it" makes sense from a design or execution perspective or not. To combat this mindset you have to be extremely forceful and proactive by offering unsolicited feedback and advice and persistently requesting to be included in key strategic meetings. While you may be concerned about ruffling feathers, all you're doing is looking for ways to make a greater contribution to your company, and who could or would even dare to take issue with that?

REACH OUT AND TOUCH SOMEONE

All of these tactics require discipline and courage and without peers to support you, you could very well give up if you meet stiff resistance. It is imperative to your success that you reach out to the creative community at large for support. There are many options open to you on both the local and national level. AIGA, HOW, InSource, local art directors and marketing organizations, and numerous websites offer opportunities to connect in powerful ways with your peers. Take advantage of them as quickly as possible. Creatives are a supportive, tight-knit group.

> You'll find others in the same situation as you who intimately understand your challenges and frustrations. Many have worked out solutions that they can share with you.

This applies not only to your business challenges but to your creative ones as well. I've spoken with many in-house creatives who routinely show their projects to their peers for creative critiques and feedback.

Make sure you acknowledge your tremendous achievements that have been accomplished under difficult circumstances, and then go out and actively improve your situation. If you don't, surely no one else will.

CHAPTER 2

Herding Cats: Client Management Made Easy

HERDING CATS

Cats are great companions and they can add joy to your life, but try putting a bunch of them in a field and getting them all to move in the same direction. Clients, like cats, can be great to partner with and can add to your professional fulfillment. Beyond these similarities to the feline species, though, is the even more important point that they are critical to the success of your projects. To take the analogy a step further, like cats, clients have a mind of their own and resist being controlled to meet your ends. As much as you may not like this fact, it is this temperament that actually makes the creative-marketing dynamic work. It creates a push-pull process, with the client constantly focused on the marketing needs and you as designer pushing for aesthetic and emotional impact. If your relationship with your clients is healthy and there is mutual respect and a shared goal of producing the best work possible, then the resulting design will successfully integrate the marketing, aesthetic and emotional priorities of the project.

The kicker is that because they're the ones controlling the project (and on whose shoulders the success of the project rests), it usually falls on you to go the extra mile and make the relationship work. It's no secret that clients often try to expand their influence on their projects beyond the marketing goals and attempt to design their projects as well. Again, it's primarily your responsibility to manage that. As much as you'd like it to be different, the fact is that it's a lot easier for them to find a new designer than for you, as an in-house designer, to find a new client.

Just to get it out of your system, here's a list of complaints (some valid, some not) that you may have about your clients:

- They're control freaks.
- They don't understand design.
- They don't understand me.
- They don't respect me.
- They abuse me with unreasonable deadlines and poor direction.
- They're incompetent.
- They only care about their careers.

Boo-hoo-hoo. You can sit around and complain about this state of affairs or you can take action—they certainly won't. Just like a cat is totally fine with being a cat, a client has no problem being a client. What follows are a number of ways to lasso in your client relationships while avoiding cat-scratch fever. Yee-ha!

RM IS THE RX:
CLIENT RELATIONSHIPS

RM, relationship management, is the cure for many of your most intractable challenges to achieving creative nirvana. It will also allow you to more effectively support your company in its marketing efforts. There is precious little coverage of this topic in design school curriculums, yet it is one of the single biggest factors that contribute to a design project's success. It's also the area that designers have the fewest innate skills (or least desire) to manage. We go into design because we like to wrestle with problems on our own or with like-minded colleagues—not because we like dealing with others telling us what to do in areas where they have no expertise.

As an in-house designer, you're in a very different position when it comes to working with clients than your agency and design studio peers. Your in-house relationship with them presents you with unique opportunities and challenges. On the downside, your clients might tend to take you and your team for granted, assume that you aren't as talented as your peers on the outside and resent the fact that they may be forced to use you. On the upside, you have nine-to-five (or -six or -seven) access to them and have excellent opportunities to bond with them in ways that designers outside of the company cannot.

One of the most powerful ways your team can support your clients is in training the new hires joining your clients' departments. You can school them, most obviously, in the creative processes and procedures that exist within your company. You have a depth and breadth of valuable institutional branding and marketing knowledge to share with them as well. It's been my experience that often new marketing staff is thrown into assignments with little or no training in a sink-or-swim situation where they're expected to succeed in spite of these challenges.

Because your group has worked on similar past projects and knows the review processes, the staff needed to implement the project, the timing and the branding history of the product, you and your team are able to support these clients in ways well beyond just providing them with the final deliverables. You become consultants, mentors and peers guiding your neophyte clients through the convoluted waters of the creative and marketing processes and procedures of your company. As such, you contribute to the success of your company's marketing efforts and build strong client relationships while doing so. Don't ever be stingy in providing this type of support just because it falls outside of your suite of responsibilities. Not only are you obligated by your overall commitment to the success of your company, but these efforts establish you as an invaluable part of your company and ensure your long-term stature and viability.

MAY I HELP YOU?
CUSTOMER SERVICE 101

Like it or not, as an in-house designer, you need to embrace the tenets of customer service. Chances are you have more direct client contact than your design peers in the agency world who have account executives to liaise with clients. This is not about brown-nosing or suffering abuse. It's about extending common courtesies, acting in a civil and professional manner, and enhancing your relationship with your client in ways that will lead to more trust and ultimately a more rewarding collaborative partnership.

Every member of your team needs to adopt this mindset. It only takes one or two bad experiences with an oppositional designer in your group to sour a client on your entire department. This means that whatever practices you've personally adopted should be shared with your peers and, if you have them, your reports as well.

PLEASE AND THANK YOU

Most of our moms and dads taught us at a very young age to say "please" and "thank you." Somehow, once we enter the workforce, those lessons seem to be ignored or forgotten. It's easy for that to happen since many of our clients and peers in other departments seem to have forgotten them as well. This shouldn't be taken as a free pass to do the same.

On a very fundamental level, these practices resonate with others. They feel respected and often will respond in kind. Below is a list of simple behaviors that take almost no time and effort but will result in great rewards.

1. In written communication, always use a salutation, even if it's just the recipient's name (mirror your clients' communication style, i.e., if they use "Hi", so should you).
2. End with a proper sign-off on all e-mails and letters.
3. Always include your contact information in written communication and phone messages.
4. Record a personalized voicemail greeting.
5. Don't use complicated abbreviations or acronyms.
6. Use the words "please" and "thank you" liberally.
7. Don't eat, type or check e-mails while you're on the phone.
8. In e-mails and memos, write in complete sentences.
9. In all written documents and e-mails, use spell-check.

STICKS AND STONES

Invariably, you're going to come into contact with abusive co-workers, clients or peers in other departments. Self-restraint is always the best tactic. I've learned much about this particular challenge from account managers I've had the privilege to work with.

One of the best sayings I've heard is, "If it feels good, don't say it." We've all been in situations where a client has been particularly nasty, and it would feel oh so good to take their misplaced criticism and place it in an area where the sun never shines. Now, you could do that, but most likely you'll either end up in your HR generalist's office or, with a client that feels even more entitled to act inappropriately toward you. And regardless of how justified your response may have been, you'll be branded with the reputation for being oppositional and hot headed.

You have alternatives, which brings me to my second account exec saying.

> Practice the three Rs: *retreat, reflect* and *respond.*

Whenever that zinger is about to slip out, either mentally or physically withdraw from the situation, think about what result you'd like to have come out of that situation and act appropriately to achieve that result. You may want to address the problem directly with the client; you may want to escalate it to your manager and HR; you may even want to ignore it. Whatever your response, it will at least be more reasoned and deliberate and will help you achieve the outcome that you really desire.

DO WHAT YOU SAY AND SAY WHAT YOU'LL DO

This behavior is so simple and essential that I shouldn't even need to mention it, but I'm continually astounded at the number of designers who make promises, don't keep them and don't even attempt to communicate that they're not going to keep them. The deadline passes and the client actually has to contact the designer to find out what's going on.

> There is no behavior that is more destructive to your professional career and your team's reputation than making a commitment and not keeping it.

If you're trying to be nice and always say "yes" even when the response should be "no," stop doing that. If you just forget your commitments, start taking notes and using "to do" lists to support your efforts at follow through. If you're acting out in a passive-aggressive attitude because of real dysfunction within your company, then either attempt to fix the dysfunctions or find a new job.

If you make a commitment in good faith but find yourself unable to honor it due to unexpected challenges, communicate that to your client—immediately. Then work out a plan B.

"NO" IS NOT AN OPTION

Being responsible about committing (or not committing) you or your team to a deliverable doesn't mean that when you can't make good on a request that you should say "no." You need to offer your client options and "no" is not an option; it's slamming a door in your client's face. The minute you say "no," you've damaged your relationship with your client.

Instead, offer alternatives. For example, if you're asked to provide three concepts for an ad in two days' time and you don't have the resources to meet that request, counter with an offer to complete the project in three days, or to submit two concepts in the requested timeframe, or to work up thumbnails for the client. If those options don't meet your client's needs, then you could offer to work with an outside vendor, though this may cost more.

> The point is to support your client in any way possible. In your client's (and your company's) eyes, if you're not part of the solution, you're part of the problem.

One note on committing to timelines and rush requests—the final measure of whether you take on a project or not is this: If you can do it without abusing your team, then do it.If the commitment will greatly damage your team's morale, add on to an already unrelenting onslaught of unreasonable requests or erode your team's work-life balance, then you should diplomatically push back.

R-E-S-P-E-C-T

You should avoid framing your relationships with your clients around the assumption that they lack respect for you or your team. It can sure feel like that every time you get a last minute request, when you receive little or no direction on a new project, when you have major changes thrown back at you on a project you thought was finalized or when you're asked to lower your fees.

> In reality, though, your clients are just responding to unreasonable pressures and requests being made of them.

They are often overworked, understaffed and overwhelmed by their jobs, and they're looking to you for help.

Your conversation with your clients should focus on their lack of respect for "the process," which they more than likely don't even know about or understand. Even more importantly, your discussion should focus on the advantages to them of following "the process."

Create a presentation and leave-behind (as well as an intranet site) that simply and clearly explain the creative process you'd like your clients to follow. Have a lunch and learn with them to review the process. Make sure to discuss how following this process allows your team to more quickly hone in on appropriate creative solutions, thus reducing costs, making your clients' lives easier and allowing them to look good in the eyes of their managers.

Determine what gaps in the process your clients should be filling and what functions you and your team are willing to take on as a value-add.

The agencies do it, so you'd better do it, too. Are you willing to assist your clients in creating a creative brief? Can you supply them with digital proofs for review with areas to make comments and send back to you, or are you even okay with taking their comments verbally and then taking the time to transcribe them in documented form to ensure you're all on the same page? The more you're willing to take on, the more valuable (read, preferable over agencies) you'll be.

At the end of the day, though, there are many functions that your clients have to perform, and it's your job to effectively articulate the advantages to your clients of taking responsibility for those functions.

INTEGRATION

Just how close do you want to be or should you be to your clients? That depends on the type of business your company is in, the complexity of the projects that you work on and the culture of your company. It also involves weighing the importance of fostering trust, collaboration and communication with your clients with the need to create and maintain a creative, vital and supportive environment for your team.

I was fascinated by the differing viewpoints on this issue that arose during an interview I conducted with Brad Weed, a design director at Microsoft, and Stanley Hainsworth, the former head of Starbucks' internal creative group.

Brad, whose staff works on software interface design, has set up his team to reside in the same physical environment as the teams that his individual designers support. From his perspective, the complexity of the projects they work on and the interdisciplinary matrixed team culture that exists in Microsoft

---

made this the obvious and most effective choice. In other words, it is more important that his designers form a strong collaborative relationship with their peers in other disciplines than among themselves.

For Stanley, on the other hand, whose team had a decidedly more marketing-focused function with a mandate to come up with highly creative, unique solutions, it made more sense to create a designer cluster where creatives could freely collaborate and play off of each other's ideas. To fulfill his team's mandate, collaboration among the designers was more important than their relationships with their clients.

The key difference is that the "clients" for the Microsoft team are more likely to be peers, while at Starbucks there is a more traditional, hierarchical client-designer relationship. Once you determine the primary type of relationship you have with your clients, you'll be in a good position to make the best choices on how integrated your team should be with the rest of the company.

One caveat: It is tempting, because of the cultural dissonance between creatives and noncreatives, to keep your team as isolated as possible from their peers. This is a dangerous mindset that can lead to, or exacerbate, poor client and peer relationships. Whatever model you implement, err on the side of greater integration. In the long run, this tact will afford your team greater independence by facilitating understanding and trust.

TRAIN YOUR CLIENTS

As much as I advocate client service, there are often times when it is appropriate to push back (diplomatically of course) and train and educate your clients. Just as you probably received little, if any, training on how to deal with clients and the world of business in design school, the marketing MBAs you're dealing with most likely didn't learn much about the creative process and how to best leverage it (and you) to meet their needs.

Their bad habits include, but are not limited to: poor marketing and creative direction (read, "I don't have time to fill out a creative brief"), unrealistic timing expectations, poor or nonexistent feedback on concept submissions and a lack of understanding of the designer's role in the creative process.

As tempting as it might be to berate them for their ignorance or assume that they're arrogant and intentionally abusive, which is usually not the case, realize that they're overworked and overwhelmed just like you. It's best to be neutral and methodically address opportunities to improve the process. No matter how their actions may annoy or infuriate you, as long as they're not abusive, you should stay focused on how things should unfold and their contribution to that process.

When receiving an incomplete, indecipherable creative brief, if you're lucky enough to even get one, don't just demand one from your clients or complain to them how hard this is making your life. Instead, speak to how the brief is an important tool for you to quickly and effectively design the piece they are hoping for. It's about you asking them to help you help them.

> If a client asks for something to be completed in an unworkably short period of time, don't use the word unreasonable, which could be interpreted as your seemingly self-serving opinion.

Use the word I just did—"unworkable"—and explain why it is unworkable. Maybe you have to prep the final files or it needs to go through another quality control check or you have to purchase the placed image now that the project has been approved. Whatever the specifics, chances are the client doesn't know about them, making it your job to educate him.

Timelines are a particularly useful tool in managing your clients. Whether it's your assigned responsibility or not, create them if no one else picks up that particular ball. Continually remind your clients of the timeline and especially their milestones. I know some designers who, as a matter of course, include the project timeline at the end of every e-mail they send out regarding that particular project.

A common gripe you may have with your clients is their seeming disregard of your e-mails. It helps to be aware that clients often have to sort through over a hundred to two hundred e-mails a day. Help them prioritize those e-mails by calling out any specific requests you may have for them and including their name in the subject line. For example a subject line might read, "Jane Client-Immediate Response Requested On Project XYZ."

Educating your clients on your role in the creative process and your expertise may be your hardest task. It's not one that will occur overnight. Your consistent professionalism in your dealings with them will help, as will the quality of your designs. Showing a keen interest in their objectives and business showcases your respect for the business your designing for and speaks to your skills beyond the actual creation of design artifacts.

Leveraging the thoughtfulness, insights and commitment of the design community as a whole to business concerns can also go a long way toward establishing and enhancing your design business credentials. Groups such as AIGA, HOW, InSource and DMI publish numerous essays, articles and white papers on the practice of design that you can offer up to your clients. These and other organizations also hold conferences and smaller events that you can bring your clients to—this helps expose them to professional designers and helps them understand the focus you bring to your work as well.

> Most importantly, how you conduct yourself in conversations regarding your projects will most directly impact your clients' perceptions of you.

If you're confident, assertive, open-minded and are focused as much on the business goals as the aesthetics of a job, you will, over time, mold your clients' perception of you into that of a strategic partner deserving of respect and attention.

CHAPTER 3

The Marketing Imperative: Sell Like Hell

MARKETING IS AS
MARKETING DOES

Marketing an in-house group is the most neglected tactic available to in-house teams to improve their standing in their company. In a 2007 AIGA in-house survey, over 60 percent of the respondents admitted to not marketing their groups. In-house teams mistakenly believe that this is unnecessary—that they have a built-in client base. Even if that's true, which it oftentimes isn't, it's important to establish and reestablish yourselves as a valuable creative resource and expand on the types of support you offer. Otherwise, when the bean counters start looking for ways to reduce overhead, your team runs the risk of being targeted as expendable.

I'm going to start with a simple list of the obvious ways to sell yourself and your team and then venture into some softer sell territory.

You can:

1. conduct lunch and learns
2. hold capabilities presentations
3. create a promotional website
4. create and distribute a promotional brochure
5. create and distribute a promotional CD
6. create a marketing campaign
7. create an e-mail blast
8. present case studies

These are the obvious tactics. In addition, though, there are a number of less obvious, but equally important, ways to sell yourself, your team and the value of design.

TELL TALL TALES

You're in an elevator when you notice you're alone with a potential client. You could sidle up to him and rattle off a bullet point list of your team's strengths: agency quality staff, state of the art Macs, efficient SOPs and project management solutions, etc., etc., etc. Chances are he'll forget everything you said within thirty seconds of exiting the elevator. Or you could relate a story about how you pulled a project that one of his co-workers gave you out of the fire. It had a ridiculously tight deadline with unclear objectives and multiple stakeholders. Your team worked with that client to address those issues and successfully deliver the materials that resulted in unprecedented sales. I'll bet the potential client will remember that pitch.

Stories that illustrate your value resonate much more powerfully with others than a laundry list of features. Hone your storytelling skills and leave the details to an e-mail follow-up or brochure.

TAKE IT PERSONALLY

There is no more powerful way to sell yourself and your group than to establish personal relationships with your clients and upper management. As much as you may want it to be about the quality of the work you produce and the value you bring to the company, human nature dictates that you need to establish personal bonds with others in your company. This generates a level of understanding, trust and mutual respect that can't be built any other way. Bonding is the currency of corporate culture, the grease that allows the engine of the creative process to chug along.

This means that you have to get out from behind your beloved monitor and press the flesh. If you are physically situated close enough to your clients to walk over and discuss an issue with them instead of picking up the phone, then walk over. Tim O'Donnell, a senior designer in the Global Strategic Design team at Johnson & Johnson, told me how he makes it a point to venture out from his team's great studio in New York to meet face to face with his clients in New Jersey on a regular basis. Though it isn't necessary for him to do that with the technological infrastructure at his disposal, he's found that it helps him in dealing with his clients on a day-to-day basis.

When disagreements arise, he's in a much better position to resolve the issues as a result of his outreach.

Lunches are a great opportunity to meet with colleagues and clients in a less formal and stressful setting. Conversations about family, personal pursuits and interests also help create mutual appreciation and inject a human element to your relationship (never a bad thing in the corporate world). These suggestions are not about buttering up the client but are about creating opportunities for you and your clients to find common ground, understand each other and have a personal stake in each other's success.

> And finally, understand and communicate your value proposition to your company.

When you're selling something, it's a good idea to know what it actually is that you're selling. For in-house teams dealing with upper management, that means selling the value that you bring to them and the company. Your management team is not primarily interested in the specifics of your group—how many computers you have, how many awards you've won or even who's on your team. What they really want to know is how the existence of your group contributes to the profitability of the company.

There are basically two ways your team impacts the company's bottom line. You either help the company make more money, or help the company save money by providing the most cost-effective option for producing marketing materials. That's it.

PROFITING FROM PROFIT

Making the case for how your team enhances the sales of the products or services your company markets is the tougher sell of the two value propositions. This is because it's hard to tease out the factors that contribute to the success of a product or service brought to market. It could be that promotional incentives, superior offerings or a cracker-jack sales force were the main drivers. There could be external factors independent of the company's efforts that impacted sales numbers.

The best way to document this value statement is to determine when new marketing materials are introduced for an existing product or service and, after a period of time, look for a spike in sales. The other, more difficult, option is to compare your company's sales upon the introduction of new marketing materials to total market share (your competitors' sales).

There are other, more nuanced, ways your team contributes to profitability. For example, even if your team doesn't create consumer pieces, arguably the collateral most responsible for enhancing sales, you might be responsible for creating killer sales aids and educational materials that empower your sales force to more effectively sell your product to retailers.

Speed to market is another area that makes you a driver of profits. Unlike outside resources that may want to add time to a project because that translates into more billable hours, you're driven to be as quick and efficient as possible. This results in getting promotional materials to market more quickly, which leads to more time in front of customers and higher sales volume.

An adjunct to this value proposition is the establishment of metrics by which the success and contributions of your team can be more easily assessed than by combing through sales reports.

> Work with upper management to gauge their expectations, turn those expectations into clear measurable goals for you and your team, and establish a timeframe and method for determining if your team meets those goals on a quarterly basis.

For example, your company may want to present the corporate brand in a more powerful and consistent manner. You and your team can propose specific strategies and tactics on how best to achieve that goal. Your group could sample and assess current corporate communications and marketing materials and work with upper management to establish and document branding standards, which would then be distributed to all internal and external groups that create those materials. Your team could also be included in the review process to ensure that the materials being reviewed meet the brand standards you established. An assessment of the program in six to twelve months, where the newer materials created after the initiative was begun are compared to older materials, will showcase how effective your team's efforts have been.

SHOW ME THE MONEY: THE IN-HOUSE COST SAVINGS RATIONALE

On the cost-savings front, you need to be able to effectively compare your costs for providing creative services to the costs of the other options that your company has access to. This can become a slippery slope if not handled correctly.

Whatever you do, do not position this conversation as addressing the value of the design function itself. By this I mean don't assign dollar amounts to design artifacts by saying, "I can get the cost for a sales brochure down to a thousand dollars! Whaddaya think!?" If you ever go down that path in discussions with your upper management, not only will you bungle your attempt to gain resources and stature for your team, you will damage the perception of the value of design and turn it into a commodity in the eyes of your business peers.

What this conversation is, is a well-reasoned, financially unassailable proposition on the value that in-house creative teams bring to their companies. It's about in-house design as a business model.

Simply put, in-house teams, when well positioned, well run and properly resourced, are more cost effective and efficient than working with outside agencies on many design projects. There are hard, as well as soft savings, though make no mistake that the soft savings result in real dollar cost efficiencies, too.

HARD SAVINGS

To document your real or potential cost efficiencies will involve some investigative legwork. You'll have to gather hard data that benchmarks your costs against those of existing or future vendors. The most basic point of comparison is hourly rates. Reach out to procurement or accounts payable to get the agency rates. For your rates, add up the salaries of all people on your team and add in an additional 35 percent for full-time employees to account for benefits. Divide the total by the number of staff on your team to get a blended annual rate per staff member. Then divide this figure by 1,920 hours (48 weeks × 40 hours). This will give you the blended hourly rate per person. (Note: 48 weeks was used to take into account vacation, holidays and sick days.) You can then present the agency/design firm costs side by side with your costs.

Be aware that this formula does not take into account overhead other than your salaries, such as office space and utilities. It therefore could be argued that you are not comparing apples to apples. If you put this formula into the context of your company's fixed operating costs, though, it actually speaks to a key advantage of having an in-house department: the leveraging of existing corporate assets to gain additional value. Simply put, it's most likely that your company has made commitments for office space and contracts for office services that, whether or not your team was there, would have to be paid for. In essence, your company is using these resources (which otherwise may have gone to waste) to better effect than paying agency rates that have to include the agency's operating overhead, such as rent and equipment.

This rationale can be extended to personnel. An outside firm has to employ staff to handle nondesign functions such as HR, bookkeeping and legal functions. Your company can leverage their existing staff in finance, HR, operations, etc., to support your team at no additional cost to their marketing budget. Taking this a step further, your in-house team's structure is most likely flatter than an outside design firm's. While they may have account executives, and traffic and project coordinators that add cost to their projects, many of these functions are likely being handled by your design staff, further reducing overhead (and possibly adding efficiencies).

Outside of illustrating the value gained by leveraging fixed corporate assets, this exercise will also highlight the fundamental fact that your team is based on a nonprofit model where you're incentivized to save money in every way possible (of course without sacrificing quality). That means that there is no markup on your hourly staff costs, that any out-of-pocket expenses are a pass-through with no handling fees being added on and that projects are not worked on a minute longer than they need to be.

SOFT SAVINGS

There are many nondesign functions your team provides that save your company money that external partners cannot provide. Your team has a broad and deep understanding of the marketing, review and creative procedures and policies established by your company. Aside from the obvious efficiencies this affords you and your company in the production of deliverables, you are also in the unique position to assist in the training and support of new marketing hires in these areas. Your team can guide your clients and other partners on how to most efficiently move their projects through the often complicated processes of project initiation, creation, review and revisions so they can be more productive by spending more time on their core strategic competencies and less on project logistics.

Your added value also includes the branding knowledge that you and your team possess. Your group will catch unintended branding and compliance errors early in the creative process before they get to a stage where it would take much more time (and money) to correct.

The faster marketing materials are produced, the greater the cost savings. Less hours spent on a particular job means lower costs. Your team's "speed to market" efficiencies and advantages over agencies include quicker learning curves than agencies on new projects, incentives to shorten turn times and greater access to clients, as well as the previously mentioned knowledge of brand and regulatory approval processes your team possesses.

In addition to accessibility, the familiarity and relationships you have with your clients affords your team insights into their needs and communication styles that not only allows you to reach design solutions more quickly but can enhance the quality of the designs as well. There are opportunities to establish levels of trust, achieved from an acknowledgment that you and your clients are both on the same team with the same goals, that can result in creative freedom and access to increased resources that would never occur in relationships with outside agencies.

Keep in mind that the two value propositions—hard and soft savings—are not mutually exclusive. Depending on the mix of deliverables that you provide to your company, you may embody both. Bottom line, though, is that this sell is about the bottom line.

BOTTOM-UP, TOP-DOWN

There's a simple but effective marketing practice unique to the corporate environment to which in-house teams should pay particular attention—the bottom-up top-down strategy. It involves carefully targeting both your clients and upper management in your selling efforts.

> You simultaneously focus on providing excellent customer service for your clients and powerfully presenting your capabilities to them while consistently communicating your value proposition to upper management.

You eventually reach a point where, through constant and effective outreach, these two key groups start to independently recognize the true value that you and your team bring to the company. Your clients realize that you have their best interests in mind and are providing excellent strategic and tactical support to their marketing efforts, and upper management begins to understand that there is truly a strategic role for you and your group in the company. You then reach critical mass, where upper management reaches out for confirmation of your value to your clients, who at this point are primed and even proactively communicating to upper management about your contributions to their marketing efforts.

Conversely, focusing only on one group greatly diminishes the effectiveness of your marketing efforts; in fact, it can be worse than not marketing your group at all. If you focus only on your clients, the danger is that while they may advocate for you and your team, their efforts at pointing out your value to your bosses will go unheeded because of a lack of appreciation and understanding of your inherent ROI. (Upper management will see you only as additional overhead and your clients' communications as motivated purely by self-interest and lacking in credibility). On the other hand, if you market solely to the VPs in your company, you run the very real danger of creating buy-in with upper management who then force your services on your unwilling clients who are not convinced of your ability to meet their needs and resent being forced to work with you.

ALL STEAK AND NO SIZZLE WILL MAKE YOUR PRESENTATION FIZZLE

Design presentations are the most powerful opportunity for you to showcase your value to the company, gain your clients' respect and sell your concept. Because of an in-house group's on-site, day-to-day dealings and familiarity with its clients, it's easy to fall into the trap of approaching these meetings with a lackadaisical attitude. Never look at a presentation as an informal meeting where you throw out color copies on the table because you just gossiped with your client at the water cooler. Your presentation is a reflection not only of how seriously you take your role in the process and your relationship with your clients, it also speaks directly to your creativity and respect for the work you've produced. If you don't care enough about your work to present it powerfully, then why should your clients take it seriously? Use these meetings as a chance to strut your stuff.

SURFACE PLEASURES

Below is a list of suggestions on how to best present the physical representations of your concepts:

1. Mount your concepts on blackboard.
2. Produce takeaway booklets of the presentation with bullet point design rationale.
3. Create a PowerPoint presentation if appropriate.
4. Print out your concepts on decent grade paper.
5. Create actual comps to better show how the finished piece will look.
6. Arrange the presentation in a way that most clearly showcases your concepts.
7. Make sure the meeting room is clean and uncluttered.
8. Use steel T-pins when posting your work on a presentation wall.
9. Set up the meetings to avoid interruptions.

MORE THAN SKIN DEEP

A presentation is a performance, so you should know your audience and craft your presentation to its style of business and position. This is no different from designing a piece to speak to a specific demographic. Just as you would use a more feminine font for a baby product piece marketed to new moms, you should tailor the way you dress and speak to the audience to whom you're presenting. If it's another creative team, you might wear jeans and funky shoes; if it's a mid-level marketing client, business casual may be in order; and if it's a high-level VP, you may even want to wear a suit—account execs from agencies do.

Beyond the skin deep nuances of your communication, there are some very important fundamental habits and behaviors to adopt when presenting.

> You need to be clear, objective, logical and concise. Speak to the ways in which your concept answers the marketing objectives of the assignment. Don't offer up a lot of personal opinions.

Prepare a carefully worked out business rationale for your concepts, but keep it simple. Use bullet points. It's important to keep in mind that, very often, your clients have to sell your concepts to their bosses without the advantage of having you there. You need to give them as much support as possible by keeping the explanations concise and impactful.

Your presentation is also an opportunity for you to enhance your relationship with your clients. Start out by thanking them for their input and contributions prior to the presentation. If they offer up suggestions, acknowledge those suggestions. By the way, acknowledgment does not mean agreement. You can thank them for wanting to help by offering their insights and still voice your disagreement to their opinions. At the end of the presentation, thank them again for their input. This helps solidify a sense of partnership and trust between you and your clients.

Above all else, your presentation is a forum for objectively assessing your design, getting feedback on how to improve the design and determining next steps. There is primarily only one way to do this effectively: Listen, question and document.

All of this is not as easy as it sounds. We designers, for better and for worse, own our work and often take criticism personally. This may make it difficult to hear what the clients are

really telling you. They may say that the logo looks too formal, but all you'll hear is "I don't like the logo," which then sinks down to "I don't like you." At this point, of course, you're going to get upset. Try to ignore that voice and the filter it throws up that prevents you from hearing what is truly being said. Don't get defensive and start spouting off all the talking points you rehearsed that have nothing to do with the feedback.

> Once you can effectively listen to your clients, you're in a good position to ask questions to clarify or get more detailed feedback from the clients on your concept.

Here you need to be a bit of a detective and mind reader. The clients often will not be able to clearly articulate their response to the work being presented. You'll need to tease it out of them.

Finally, don't rely on your memory to hold all the feedback you get. Either write down the feedback yourself or have someone else from your team do so. Afterwards, send a recap to your client to confirm you understood his feedback. Use the recap as an opportunity to advise next steps and timing.

PRACTICE MAKES PRESENTATION PERFECT

This is pretty self-explanatory. For any presentation of a mid- or high-level project, make sure to rehearse what you're going to say and how you're going to say it—out loud, not just in your head. If the talk is super-duper high level, you may even want to have a co-worker throw anticipated questions or concerns at you. Use props and, if possible, rehearse in the room where you're actually going to make the presentation. Make sure to get to the room early to set up your equipment and boards.

Presentations are rich with opportunities to accomplish multiple goals of creative buy-in, acquire respect for you and your team and gain useful feedback to improve your work.

CHAPTER 4

It's All About You

WHO YOU ARE MATTERS

Who you are, and how you choose to perceive your working environment—and then behave in it—is more important to your in-house professional success than your design skills. As a matter of fact, those attributes directly impact the quality of your design projects. If you act in a way that disrupts or subverts the collaborative process, or causes your clients and managers to distrust you or your peers to avoid you, your designs will suffer. There are four important points to remember:

1. It's not enough just to be a good designer when working in-house.
2. It's not enough to satisfy your creative muse through the practice of design.
3. It's not enough to coast through your job.
4. And it's definitely not enough to skirt the big issues regarding your career and blow off taking the time to really determine what you want in your professional life.

As an in-house designer, you need skills that your peers in agencies and studios don't. Given that you will most likely be interfacing with nondesigners on a daily basis, there are interpersonal and business communication competencies and habits that are essential to your success. Some include decent writing skills, the ability to articulate your thoughts in meetings, project management expertise and infinite patience. (See chapter five.)

Don't look to your job as a source of creative expression and fulfillment. Your job is not about being self-expressed; it is about solving problems using your craft and insights. That doesn't mean it won't be enjoyable, but designing certainly doesn't scratch the same itch as painting, drawing or sculpting does.

When your job beats you down or your clients disrespect you, when you get little support from upper management, and all your peers are constantly complaining, it's easy to throw in the towel and become just another apathetic disaffected in-house designer. If you're unfortunate enough to get to that point, you should either quit or start taking positive action to improve your environment. Otherwise, you'll end up far worse professionally, creatively and personally. There are many suggestions in this book on how to improve your environment. If you act like a victim, guess what? You'll be a victim.

Most importantly, take time to figure out what your priorities are. If they're creative freedom, peer recognition, money, flexibility and self-employment or owning your own business, then the agency/studio world may be the best choice for you. If you enjoy working with multidisciplinary teams, you like financial stability, strive for a work/life balance and find fulfillment in making significant but incremental changes to an organization, then in-house is for you. Don't go through this process alone. Besides the obvious choice of working this through with your significant other, it's good to go through this exercise with a peer designer and an older experienced creative for additional perspective and insights.

BE A CREATIVE CONSULTANT

Never look at yourself as just a designer. It limits your ability to contribute to your company and limits how your peers and clients view you. There are many other ways that you can support your company and garner respect for yourself and your team in the process. Some include:

- managing agency relationships
- consulting on printing and agency contracts
- visualizing abstract business concepts for peer teams
- assisting other teams in brainstorming and creative collaboration
- contributing to marketing strategy and insights

The opportunities for you to bring your expertise to bear on problems outside of the creation of designed materials is only as narrow as your definition of yourself and how you fit into the company where you work. More importantly, you think differently than your nondesign peers and can contribute perspectives and insights on nondesign problems that will be innovative and valuable.

WHAT WOULD
MACHIAVELLI DO?

Navigating the maze of the corporate political landscape
demands a way of thinking about your business that you may
not normally be inclined to do. "Why play those games?" you
may ask. After all, if you and your team do good work and
effectively service your clients, shouldn't you be guaranteed
a position of respect and value within your company? Well ...
how can I say this? No.

The reality is that your success and value are a matter of
perceptions as well as truths. In addition, the competing interests of different individuals, departments and business units
can mow down even the most productive of creative teams.

Clients will, at times, sacrifice the good of the company for
their own professional gain. That may mean clients choosing
to work with agencies assuring that there is less transparency
of their projects being afforded to their managers and financial

peers. This way, if mistakes are made, they will not be recognized by upper management.

You may have a great idea that would contribute to the overall efficiency and productivity of your team, yet your manager may rebuff you, not wanting to risk a failure that could tarnish their lackluster but safe reputation.

The list of obstacles is long, so someone on your team has to take a look at how you fit into your company, whom to ally yourselves with and where best to look for funding. This could mean doing business favors (not personal favors!) for individuals in a good position to support your team. It might mean looking for funding in budgets that are untouchable by the bean counters (probably marketing dollars—not operations or administrative budgets). You may need to jockey your team so that it reports to a manager who has clout with the C-level executives to ensure your group's long-term viability.

As uncomfortable, unfamiliar or downright distasteful as this practice may be, given the current state of affairs in most companies, it is an essential undertaking (in as limited a degree as possible) for you and your team's success.

MANAGE UP AND DOWN

As a designer who is in a profession that creates and values artifacts, you most likely assume that the recognition of the value and contributions that you bring to your companies will be based on your work. If you're a design team leader, chances are you've adopted this mindset in a slightly modified form and applied it to your managerial responsibilities. The assumption goes something like, "I don't really need to interact much with upper management. If I spend my time and my efforts on developing and nurturing my team to a point where they're producing great creative work on time and within budget, upper management will value and support my team and me." This is one of the biggest mistakes you can make as a manager.

Your manager and your manager's manager most likely have no idea what you and your team do nor how you and your team do it. If you're lucky, their background may be in marketing, but your manager is just as likely to have come from a business, finance, operations or, heaven forbid, HR area of expertise. He will only understand (and value) your team through his interactions and communications with you.

> It is therefore imperative that you manage up as well as down. Developing a mutually respectful, trusting, communicative relationship with your management team is the best way to ensure that you and your fellow creatives are valued and supported.

Whether the needs your managers express are design related or not, it's incumbent upon you to meet those needs, and then some. Don't come to them with problems without also having a proposed solution. Don't complain—explain. Your job is to make them look good. Your job is to support them. Your job is to make their life easier. And if you're lucky and you have a good manager, he'll do the same for you.

DEVELOP SKILLSETS

There's not a lot to elaborate on regarding the unique in-house skills you need beyond the list below. Of course, different in-house teams have different staffing structures and mandates regarding services and deliverables, so not everything on this list may apply to you.

You should possess:

- strong writing skills
- good verbal and presentation skills
- the ability to multitask
- a hide as thick as a rhino's
- excellent keyboard skills
- an excellent, slightly sardonic, sense of humor
- excellent organizational skills
- ability to interface with vendors
- ability to interface with clients (without resorting to violence)
- infinite patience for bureaucratic exchanges
- a backbone to challenge inane or destructive corporate policies and procedures
- the perseverance of a madman
- the ability to be creative under severe compliance and marketing restraints
- a love, passion and respect for design so strong, people get caught up in your enthusiasm

37 SURE-FIRE
WAYS TO GET FIRED...

Undoubtedly, the quality of your creative problem-solving skills, insights and final deliverables are the primary determinants of your professional success. Equally important in the corporate setting, though, are your communication, interpersonal and collaborative skills as well as your attitude, temperament and mindset. I can recall times I've helplessly watched excellent creatives crash and burn because they didn't practice proper business and personal etiquette. Some were incapable of understanding the rules, some were dead set against following the rules and some just didn't care. It's critical to understand that how you choose (or not) to conduct yourself in your relationships with your clients, peers and companies is more than just greasing the wheels of corporate politics—those behaviors are actually absolutely essential to the process of creating effectively designed materials for your companies.

Conversely, there are times when corporate policies can compromise you and your team's creativity, productivity, integrity and even humanity. Sometimes logic and simple decency buckle under the quest for efficiency (read, standardization) or legal priorities of companies. It can feel as if you've walked through Alice's looking-glass and the very behaviors and practices that should be rewarded or condemned become inverted. At that point it's best to push back and assert yourself even if it means confrontation and possible dismissal. No job, no position, no title is worth giving up your ideals and beliefs.

That being said, there are ways to stand up for what you believe in that are effective, and there are ways that are potentially self-destructive. Some ways will empower you to transform yourself, your colleagues and your work environment. Others will piss off your peers and upper management and at best get you fired, at worst leave you working in a hostile environment. The aim of this chapter is to offer strategies and tactics that will support you in the former and help you avoid the latter. To do that I'm serving up ways to get fired in the hopes that you'll NOT try these at work. (However, if you're truly miserable and want to get out, by all means give them a try.) Then I'll list ways to break rules in order to succeed where your corporations might be unintentionally setting you up to fail.

PISS OFF YOUR CLIENTS

1. Avoid your clients. When they call, don't answer the phone. Leave messages only when you know they're not there. Don't respond to e-mails and don't talk to them when you see them in the halls. Never ever have lunch with them.

2. Be rude and abrupt in the few communications you do have with them. Don't use proper salutations in your e-mails. Don't say "please" or "thank you." Keep your sentences short and grammatically incorrect and add numerous misspellings lest they think you care enough about them to use spell check. Never sign your e-mails or leave your contact info in a voicemail. Bonus tip: Eat and type on your keyboard while you're on the phone.

3. Interrupt your clients when they're giving you direction or feedback. Know they have nothing of value to offer. If they do get a word in, shoot them a disdainful and dismissive look.

4. Miss deadlines. Need I say more on this point?

5. Say "no" as much as possible. NEVER say "yes"—just sigh and, if they happen to be in the room with you, roll your eyes for added effect.

6. Bad mouth your clients to others in your company. Complain about their lack of understanding of design and that they're control freaks (which you, of course, are not).

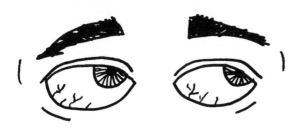

7. Don't ever try to assist your clients with issues outside of design. If they don't understand the routing or review process, don't explain it to them. If they don't know how to cut a PO for your outside vendor, never let on that you have the document from finance that explains how. It is not your job to help them in these areas.

8. When something goes wrong on a project, never accept responsibility for it. Do your best to make it the client's fault.

9. Talk to your clients like you would talk to your friends at a party. Address them as "dude." Mumble, ramble and speak in one-word sentences. You shouldn't have to change who you are by speaking their language—you're a designer, not a suit!

10. Don't give the client what they asked for. Go off brief: It was wrong anyway.

11. Throw around lots of design terms that they don't understand. It's not your problem if they don't know kerning from leading. Aren't they in marketing? Didn't they learn anything about design in business school?

12. Don't design effective pieces for clients you don't like—they don't deserve the best of your talents and neither does the company for being stupid enough to have hired them in the first place.

13. Be late to meetings—all the time. Better yet, don't go at all. Meetings are a total waste of your time.

PISS OFF YOUR FELLOW DESIGNERS AND MANAGERS

14. Make it all about you. Take credit for as much as you can (and more). Never share credit with others. Bonus tip: Do not participate in any team-building events, departmental social gatherings or new staff welcomes or leaving staff send-offs.

15. Work on freelance projects on company time. If your manager can't keep you busy, that's her problem. Never offer to take on a long-term project such as archiving all your stock images.

16. Complain about your peers to your fellow designers, managers and staff in other departments.

17. Never do any work that you can pass off to a more junior member of your team.

18. Keep personal files on the company workstation—especially pirated music and movies.

19. Hand off files that are a complete mess to your production artists. Use lo-res images, apply font styles in your layout programs and don't include dielines or correct dimensions, etc.

20. Use company resources for personal use. Send personal FedExes, make personal long distance calls (preferably international) and use company printers for your yard sale posters.

21. Complain to your manager as much as possible and never offer up solutions—that's his job as your manager.

22. Never work overtime no matter how critical the project is. Your manager gets paid more than you; let her give up a Saturday afternoon.

23. Leapfrog over your manager to your one-up manager when you have a disagreement. Make sure to bad mouth your manager when doing so.

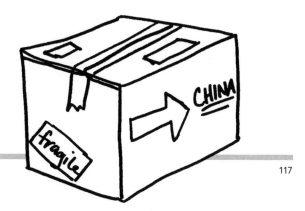

24. Dis your co-workers, managers and company on your Facebook page. No one you work with would ever find it, and even if they did, you weren't posting to it on company time so it's a private affair. Isn't it??? Bonus tip: Start a blog about work and invite all your co-workers to join in the fun. This will help them get fired, too!

25. Send inappropriate e-mails from your work e-mail account. Cram as many sex jokes, ethnic slurs and links to porn sites into your missives to friends as you can.

26. Leapfrog your team and contact the client directly without your peers' knowledge or consent. You need to get the project done, project manager be damned.

27. Create folders on your workstation with titles like "Bullsh$%@t" and put company notices, promotion announcements and departmental policy e-mails in it.

28. Be a yes-man. Never offer up ideas that may challenge your peers or your manager. Make sure they know you're a brown-noser by nodding in constant agreement as vigorously as a bobble-head on the dashboard of a Jeep. This may not get you fired, but you'll be first in line at layoff time.

29. Be uncoachable. Brush off anyone's attempt to offer you constructive criticism and support. Be defensive. Act like a know-it-all. Argue with those trying to help you.

ADOPT BAD DESIGN HABITS

30. Pay more attention to the brand than your audience. It's all about the logo and the brand style guide. Who cares if the design resonates with your company's customers or not?

31. Don't worry about whether the piece is printable or not—that's the printer's problem.

32. Don't be concerned about whether the design meets the client's objectives—focus only on whether it will be a good piece for your portfolio.

33. Forget about marketing materials compliance—or any compliance for that matter. These inane policies are a

waste of your time and take the fun out of design. If the company gets sued, the lawyers will handle it. That's what they're paid for.

34. Abuse your vendors.

35. Don't stay current on your apps. Fall behind your peers in your understanding of the applications you work on every day. Your co-workers can always open your legacy files and, if the fonts and images convert incorrectly, well, that's their problem.

BE ARROGANT AND APATHETIC

36. Always, always make everyone else wrong and let everyone else know that you're right. This applies to your company, your co-workers, fellow designers, managers, upper management, and clients—and for an added effect, apply it to your family and friends, too! Nothing you can do is more effective at angering people and making you a pariah (resulting in getting canned) than asserting your rightness and everyone else's wrongness.

37. Be apathetic. Have absolutely no passion for your craft, your peers, your company or your job. Know you should be someplace better than where you are right now.

... AND 13 STANDS WORTH
THE RISK OF THE PINK SLIP

There are times when it's appropriate to push the envelope and possibly risk getting yourself fired. If you challenge the status quo with a clear and positive rationale, you may effect needed change within your company and minimize the possibility of termination. Use your judgment, but chances are, that gnawing feeling in your gut that something is just not right will be your best guide on when and how to take a stand.

TAKE A STANCE AGAINST HUMAN RESOURCES POLICIES

1. Fight with HR for the highest salaries you can get for your team. Often HR tries to find seemingly comparable positions that exist within the company to use as a measure for your group's positions. There are none, though they'll go through contortions of logic to convince themselves that there are. Use whatever resources you have available to you—particularly professional organizations' salary research—to make your case that a mid-level accountant's salary should not be used to benchmark a junior designer's compensation. You have to be competitive within the industry—not your company—to attract good talent.

2. Refuse to use—or at least amend—your HR-mandated interview process when staffing up your team. The stan-

dard questions for determining good mid-level managers in finance, HR, compliance and manufacturing have almost no relevance to the practice of design. Discuss the primary functions and skills of designers and other creatives on your team with your HR staffing specialist and compare them to the corporate interview process. Illustrate the disconnect and how that disconnect could jeopardize your ability in determining appropriate hires.

3. The same issues in no. 2 apply to performance reviews. Take the same stance after determining the metrics you believe should be used.

4. Push back on HR when your instincts tell you HR is advocating a response you know is inappropriate—trust your gut. HR can get pretty wacky when it comes to compliance issues. Follow your moral compass and instincts, not theirs, in determining if the correct actions are being taken in response to a team member's transgression. Be assertive and persistent in addressing any differences of opinion in these matters and DOCUMENT EVERYTHING.

FIGHT THE BUREAUCRATIC BEAST

5. It is always easier to ask for forgiveness than permission, no matter what the issue or need—period.

6. Tear down the walls. If you have special space requirements, build a case for them and don't give up until you get what

you want. The design process presents unique needs for collaboration and presentation, and because design results in the creation of physical pieces, we often need additional space for reviewing and storing press proofs and comps.

7. Say "thank you" your way. Companies often restrict managers' options to reward their staffs for hard work. Comp days are a big source of conflict with creatives who are frequently called upon to work late hours to meet deadlines, and their managers are not permitted to compensate them for those hours. I, and other managers I've spoken with, have provided off-site "research days" to their teams as a work-around.

8. Bend the rules. While compliance serves a very important purpose in the corporate world, there are times when, given the unique expectations placed on your team, they can become an impediment. Use common sense. Don't ever put your company at risk legally or ethically, but if you're at a juncture where the success of a project means circumventing a well-intentioned but low-level risk-averse policy, you may want to bend the rules.

9. Fight for your freedom of choice. There is a rationale for restricting the vendors a corporate department can use—it just doesn't happen to work for creative teams. This problem arises because the myriad of outside service providers creative groups need to partner with don't neatly fit into the purchasing department's predefined categories. Enroll your clients as allies to support you in working with or circumventing purchasing when these conflicts arise.

10. Get your company to play nice with your vendors. The single biggest cause of sour relationships with vendors is accounts payable. They throw up infuriating process and procedural roadblocks to getting your vendors paid in a timely manner. You need to be a thorn in their side to ensure that your outside partners are fairly and expeditiously paid for their services.

11. Push the envelope wisely. As an entrepreneurial group trying to function in the corporate environment, you're confronted with having to push the policy envelope on

a daily basis to meet your clients' needs. The nine-mph-over principle is a good practice to follow. Generally, you can drive a little more quickly than the posted speed limit without risking a ticket by only going nine miles per hour over the limit. Anything more greatly increases your risk. The same applies to following corporate policies and procedures. Use your judgment to mitigate the possibility of anything more than a slap on the wrist.

12. Don't let IT force you to adopt their tools and protocols. Fight to bring in Mac consultants if they don't possess that expertise.

13. Do not allow yourself to be set up to fail. This is the most important issue to risk getting fired for. Unenlightened upper management may cut back on your resources and still expect you to complete your tasks. They may even pile new responsibilities onto your plate. You're then at a crossroads. Do you complain and even refuse to step up and deliver, or keep quiet, hunker down and watch your quality of life and the quality of your performance suffer? The hunker down option is a short-term self-defeating fix because you will eventually fail either due to exhaustion or alienation and disgust. Not a good way to make an exit. Better to honestly, objectively and honorably forcefully articulate the unsustainability of your situation. If you get fired at least it will have been for taking a principled stand.

YOU'RE FIRED: PLAN ON IT

During a workshop I gave called "In-house Intrapreneurialism," I asked the participants if they were willing to be fired. The context I had attempted to set up was that in order to achieve certain goals to better their teams' and their own professional lives, in-house team leaders might need to take actions that could get them fired. So, were they willing to take that risk to achieve those goals?

When few people raised their hands, I expressed surprise and self-righteously pronounced that I had been fired as a result of my actions to better my team's working situation. A very honest woman in the group asked if I was single at the time I had placed myself at risk. I puffed up my ego and declared that not only did I have two children at the time, I had a mortgage as well. "It's not the mortgage," the woman replied, "I wanted to know if you had children." It was obvious that she did, and it occurred to me that this was something she was clearly, and of course correctly, not willing to put at risk. I fumbled about for a moment and responded somewhat lamely that no one should look to be fired and that we all need to pick our battles.

Afterwards, I was troubled by my response in that exchange, and it occurred to me that there was a much more relevant and helpful answer I could have given. I believe that the woman's priorities were completely appropriate, but I believe she had set up a false choice: taking justifiable risks at work versus the security of her children. The assumption was that if she got fired, she would not be able to provide for herself or her family. While this is a real possibility, there are ways to mitigate this risk by planning ahead to ensure a successful transition to another job if she got a pink slip. What my answer should have been was that we all should prepare for being fired to free ourselves from that fear and thus empower ourselves to behave in our jobs in ways that best serve our teams and us.

Fortunately, there are actually many ways to plan for the possibility of getting fired. The most obvious is to keep your résumé and portfolio current. A twist on this is to create multiple résumés and portfolios tailored to different types of positions or industries. A résumé for an in-house position should focus on different areas of expertise than a résumé for an agency. If you've worked in multiple industries (a good career move if you haven't already done so), you can prepare multiple portfolios that have pieces relevant to those industries. Have at least three case studies at the ready in addition to your portfolio and résumé. The case study should include a description of the goals

of the project, how the project was executed and the outcome or results (how your solution met the client's goals).

- Create a website that includes samples of your work, a bio, a résumé and other relevant information about yourself. Make sure the design of the site showcases your talent. Include the URL on all promotional pieces and communications.

- Have a brand identity for yourself designed and ready to launch on business cards, letterhead, e-mail signatures, résumés and your website.

- Establish relationships with recruiters, both permanent and temp agencies, up front. Don't wait to be fired to start looking for firms that are a good fit for you. Be willing to become a contract worker even if only temporarily. Many temp gigs turn into full-time opportunities, or you may find that you like the temp design lifestyle. One note: I've noticed a trend in corporations to staff up with full-time contract employees.

- Network like a maniac. Join industry organizations such as AIGA, InSource, Graphic Artists Guild and the Design Management Institute. Go to conferences. Stay in touch with former coworkers. More jobs are found through these types of connections than by responding to employment ads.

- But don't rule out Monster.com, CareerBuilder.com and other employment sites. Register with them now. They'll give you a sense of what's going on in our industry. You may even want to take courses to bone up on skills you don't have that you notice are in demand.

- Publish and speak on topics of interest to you and the design industry. Write articles for design publications, newsletters, websites and blogs. Present to smaller regional groups and then larger conferences. This looks good on your résumé, helps you network and trains you in how to organize your thoughts and present them effectively (good skills when you're interviewing).

- Put aside money as a cushion. This may not be possible, but if you're contributing to an IRA or 401K, know that you can tap into this money if need be, though it should be an absolute last resort.

- Make sure you have an understanding of your rights, both with your company and the government, when it comes to severance and unemployment compensation.

- However the firing is handled, conduct yourself graciously and professionally. Former co-workers who witness your exit may one day be hiring managers.

Finally, have faith in yourself and your resourcefulness. As a designer, you're trained in two key areas that will give you an advantage in finding a new job over others not in the field of design. You're trained to be a problem solver and to promote ideas, services and products. Whatever you did for your company, you can do for yourself.

> Trust, rely on and employ those skills, and you'll be positioned to successfully find a new job.

You just need to do it, and regardless of your current employment situation, you need to do it now.

CHAPTER 5

Can You Hear
Me Now?
Communication
Is Key

IT'S ALL IN THE DELIVERY

Most business communications are not about self-expression. Save that for your personal work and when you're hanging with friends and family. Business communications are about exchanging ideas and information and making requests in a way that powerfully resonate with your audience. Leave the vernacular and slang at the conference room door (unless that will positively impact your audience).

It's critical to remember that your delivery is as important or sometimes more important than what you're saying. To ensure powerful communication, you have to know your audience and tailor your style to it. Just like you use different fonts, colors and imagery in your designs depending on your target demographic, you should choose your words, body language and tonality just as carefully when speaking with someone in a business setting.

THE POWER OF LISTENING, OR, LEND THEM YOUR EARS

Without exception, whenever you're having a conversation with someone at any time, in any place, about anything, there are two people talking to you. There's the person who is physically in front of you speaking to you, and then there's the person yammering in your head—you know, the one who's commenting on everything coming out of the mouth of the person you're talking with.

> To succeed as an in-house designer, you have to tell the person in your head to shut up.

You can talk to him later. In the course of a conversation, you need to clearly hear what your peer, manager or client is saying to you at the moment she's saying it. Otherwise, any action you take, whether it's design or business related, might very well not be addressing what is really going on, but rather what you've decided is going on.

The most obvious example of this occurs when getting feedback from a client on a design project. They say, "The logo is too small." You hear, "The layout sucks." Or, "You're a lousy designer." Or, worse, "I don't like what you did because I want to control this entire project." None of which would be good to act upon. Stay focused on the exact words you're hearing and precisely respond to those words. Which brings us to…

LEARN CORPORATESE

In no other organized group is a person's means of communication governed by the adherence to such a dysfunctional lexicon of ambiguity, double-speak, veiled barbs and insults as occurs within a corporation. It is the antithesis of the "say what you mean and mean what you say" adage.

Designers are notoriously poor practitioners of this form of communication that I call *corporatese*. We're all about straight talk. When we're getting direction on a design project, we often need to work through the ambiguity in our client and peer exchanges to get the information we can use for proper execution. Designers also tend to wear their hearts on their sleeves.

Corporatese, though, is an essential tool in managing relationships with others in your company. So, bite your tongue and substitute this new language for some of the more honest but politically incorrect communications you'd like to (but shouldn't) have.

To school yourself up, pay attention to the e-mails and verbal communications of others who have a flair for corporatese. Total immersion is the only way to pick up this flair. I've included examples of this language below.

"I appreciate your input, but I don't believe it meets the marketing objectives of this initiative."
Translated: "Your idea sucks."

"That's an interesting idea and a relevant piece of feedback, but we're already up against a tight deadline."
Translated: "Shut up."

"I've reached out to the team to assess our resources to meet the needs of your project, and we can't honor your request without compromising other deadlines."
Translated: "No can do. Are you out of your mind?"

I'd recommend that, as fluent as you might get in corporatese, you use it judiciously, sparingly and cautiously. If you wield it as a weapon, you will only poison your relationships with others in the long run for the sake of short-term gains.

> It's best to use your awareness of corporatese as an opportunity to read between the lines of communications that you receive, and respond appropriately and without malice.

THE THREE SPHERES OF CORPORATE COMMUNICATION

There are three basic types of communication you engage in as an employee of a company—the selling communication, the logistical communication and the buying communication. They all have specific purposes and associated methods of delivery. These communications are the most powerful tools at your disposal in effecting positive change for you and your team. They are part of the creative process, are essential to enhancing and maintaining your standing within the company and are integral to promoting the value of design within your company. So pull this sword from the stone and start swinging.

THE SELLING COMMUNICATION: HAVE I GOT A DESIGN FOR YOU!

Any conversation you have where the purpose is to convince someone to adopt your design, strategy or business proposal should be considered a selling conversation. The tone of the delivery needs to be animated but controlled, assertive yet respectful and objective but also passionate. It's important to engage and not talk down to or speak at the person you're pitching to. And you need to listen and respond very carefully to concerns that your audience may bring up.

The Team Sell

To upper management, your department is a strategy, not a group of people; sell it that way. When you're in a sell conversation about your team, be aware that most likely the person that you're selling to has little interest in the number of people in your team, their expertise, the awards you've won, the state-of-the-art equipment you have or your tight SOPs. What they care about is how your team contributes to their personal and the corporate objectives and goals. If it's cost savings, then you need to speak to that; if it's commitment to quality, then you need to articulate how your team executes on that goal. Speak to how your team contributes to the company in ways that your audience will value.

To better explain how to make this sell consider the American Marketing Association's features/advantages/benefits method. Every sell can be approached by focusing on the features of the product or service, the advantages that result from those features or the benefits to the buyer of the advantages (or a combination of the three). Specific to your team, you could describe, as noted above, the facts about your team which will have little or no impact on your audience that is most likely made up of marketers, finance staff or MBA middle managers. You could speak to how the talent, equipment and disciplined processes contribute to faster turn times, higher quality deliverables and lower hourly rates—in other words, the advantages. Most importantly, you can present the benefits that follow from the advantages: lower costs due to the in-house, nonprofit model, faster turn times (less hours per project), higher profits due to increasing selling time by getting advertising materials to market faster, and increased sales due to higher quality design, which powerfully impacts the targeted consumer. Additional benefits to your clients might include the ability to use the saved dollars for additional marketing initiatives or other needed resources, and by putting in-house groups in the mix, agencies are compelled to be more price competitive.

In supporting your departmental sell, there are a few other points to keep in mind. It's important to be aware of your value proposition and be able to articulate it, as noted in chapter three. Speak about other in-house teams that have successfully supported their companies; it legitimizes your group to be able to reinforce the value of the in-house model. Speak in the language of your audience: It's all about ROI. Finally, sell yourself. Unless your audience trusts you personally as the face of your team, it won't even hear what you're trying to sell them.

The Design Sell

One of the hardest roles for you as a designer to take on is being the salesperson for your creative work. Aside from the knee-jerk assumption that good work should sell itself (it doesn't), you're going to be presenting an idea or artifact that you created, that is a part of you and that you're emotionally attached to. In spite of all the powerful forces that could lead you to be overly emotional, close-minded or assertive, you need to be exceptionally calm, objective and flexible. Simply put, you need to:

• Keep the focus on how the work meets the client's objectives.

- Listen carefully to concerns that are raised and address them with specificity.
- Create a partnership with your client by acknowledging their contributions to the creative process before, during and after the presentation.

To elaborate, when selling a project, keep the focus on how the design meets the marketing objectives, not the process used to create the design. Only go into the process when prompted by a client's concerns about research, ideation, etc. The creative brief is your bible! Refer to it often when discussing the intentions behind your design.

It's easy to get emotionally sidetracked and defensive when clients criticize your work. Listen to exactly what the clients are saying, attempt to dispassionately interpret it and respond to the question by addressing their specific concerns.

Give the clients talking points they can use to present to their bosses. Describe the rationale and thinking behind the design of the project so that the clients can absorb and digest it. This will give them the tools they need to sell it higher up the management chain.

Twenty Questions

To continue with the previous example, let's say your client commented that the logo was too small and you actually heard that (good for you!). Just because that's what the client said, it's not necessarily articulating what the real problem is for them. It may be that the logo, from a marketing perspective, isn't prominent enough, but their knee-jerk reaction is to make it bigger. In other words, they've offered up a solution to a problem that they haven't articulated. You need to clarify for the both of you what the client is driving at. If it's that the logo isn't prominent enough, then there are a variety of solutions other than just making it bigger that would address that issue. If it is that the client specifically wants the logo bigger and you believe that is not a good idea, then you have to steer the conversation toward identifying the underlying problem or missed objective that is driving the client's attempt at giving you a solution. By identifying the actual problem, you can explain that there are other more effective graphic solutions than simply making the logo bigger.

Below is a hypothetical conversation to help illustrate this point.

Designer: What do you think of the layout for our new product launch ad?

Client: I don't like it.

Designer: Why is that? Is it not meeting the marketing objective?

Client: It's just not focused.

Designer: Do you mean it's too busy?

Client: No.

Designer: Do you mean the picture isn't big enough?

Client: Yeah, yeah, the picture should be bigger. And, and the headline needs to be at the top of the image, not below it.

Designer: Do you mean you want the headline to be more prominent? Because there are other ways to do that besides moving it, which might clutter the layout …

(Note the number of question marks. This conversation is less about offering solutions and more about defining the problems that need to be addressed.)

Be Objective About the Objective

Whenever your client starts to art direct, move the conversation back to the marketing goals of the project. In other words, objectively address the objectives of the project. In a very matter-of-fact way, you should determine if the goal of the piece is to re-establish the company's brand or play up the new product introduction. If it's to focus on the product, then making the company logo larger runs counter to what the marketing focus of the piece should be. If there's a middle ground that needs to be reached, at least it will be driven by a common marketing goal and will keep subjectivity and personal conflict out of the conversation. The conversation should never be about you or your client and what either of you personally want. It should always be about what you're attempting to accomplish with the design. This sets up a collaborative relationship on which you can build upon to achieve the best design possible.

THE LOGISTICAL CONVERSATION: HERE'S THE INFO

Many of the conversations you have in the corporate setting involve the exchange of information, pure and simple. Well, maybe not so simple. Many, if not most screw-ups—missed deadlines, off-target creative, incorrect production and busted budgets—can trace their origins to poor communication of the factual elements of a project.

It's easy to take this type of communication for granted. In your complacency, you can get sloppy, fall into bad habits or neglect developing good habits. The good news is that, with a little discipline, this type of communication is the easiest to master.

Make a Note of It

A ton of information is thrown at you on a daily basis. With all the design-based logistics involved with your projects, not to mention the legal, branding and regulatory mandates, the only way to keep track of it all is to take notes. Never go to a meeting without pad and pen, and never assume you or someone else will remember everything that's discussed. Make a point of recapping meetings and sending out an e-mail for confirmation of accuracy to all those involved in a particular project. It's an especially good idea to do that after a phone or casual face-to-face conversation. This gives you, your client and your team an opportunity to make sure you're all on the same page, and serves as a reference point should misunderstandings arise in the future. It also lets your client know you're in charge and on the case and that you value their input.

Just the Facts Ma'am: Who, What, Why, How, Where, When
Do not start a job until the questions *who, what, where, when, how* and sometimes *why* are answered or have been committed

to being answered by your client. Nine times out of ten, if you don't get closure on these questions, you will pay the price in overtime, cost overruns and mistakes at the tail end of your job. It takes a ton of discipline to adhere to this rule.

Equally important, make sure that the answers are specific. "Soon," "ASAP" and "quickly" are not on a calendar. Even being given a specific day as a deadline can get you into trouble. Your Friday due date might mean to you 5 P.M. on that Friday, whereas your client could very well be assuming that you'll have the job done in time for their 10 A.M. presentation.

At this point, you're probably thinking, "Yeah, I'll get that info in some parallel universe where clients obey my every command and fonts load perfectly every time I open an old Quark file." There are ways to address this challenge, though. Some in-house groups have implemented a digital project initiation solution that requires certain fields be filled in before allowing the client to submit the request. Having the client fill in as much as they're willing to and then following up with a call to have them dictate to you the additional information is another option. If all else fails, fill in what you believe to be the correct information, make up a due date and other criteria that works for you and send it to your client for approval. Also see "R-E-S-P-E-C-T" in chapter two.

Over-Communicate

This may sound counterintuitive to designers who want, and should, maintain control of their projects, but over-communicating with your client may be the best way to achieve creative independence. If you think about it, when you huddle behind your monitor and come out only when (a) you have to present concepts to your client, or (b) when you fall behind but are afraid to let your client know, or (c) when you have questions about a project that arise as you delve more deeply into the project but you don't reach out to your client for fear that they'll seize control of the design, then your client is going to feel that they have no control over the outcome and react to the fear that it may fail. They'll call and e-mail you to make sure everything is going as planned. They'll trot over to your cube, and they'll call your manager and co-workers when they can't find you. None of that is what you want to happen.

Instead, make an effort to keep your client abreast of your progress, involve them when appropriate in the creative process, and if you've hit a snag either creatively or in meeting a deadline, contact them immediately. If you manage the relationship in a disciplined manner, making sure that you only ask for marketing feedback or logistical advice (as opposed to design input), you'll find that keeping your client in the loop will build a bond of trust between you and them and that, over time, they will be much more comfortable and inclined to leave you alone.

THE BUYING CONVERSATION: GET WHAT YOU NEED

Whenever you're trying to get something from a peer, an upper manager or a report, whether it's material such as money, equipment or staff, or ethereal such as respect, agreement or permission, you are engaged in a buying conversation. You are attempting to purchase acquiescence from another and the currency is your words and ideas.

As designers, we're generally not wired to effectively engage in this type of communication. The buy conversations have the potential to be emotionally charged, and as creatives, we're inclined to wear our hearts on our sleeves, which is not the best tactic in these situations.

What's In It for Them?

There is only one tact to take when engaging in the buy conversation. It is to powerfully articulate to the persons from whom you're attempting to buy something what's in it for them if they give you what you're asking for.

What's in it for them could be altruistic. It might be that what they want is to support you and your team, or they want to improve the culture in your company or they believe in the value of design. It could also, of course, be that they have an agenda of self-promotion, a desire for power and a need to dominate their fellow managers. Whatever their reasons are, you need to be aware of them.

So when you're talking to someone about what you want and need for you and your team, don't talk about your pain and don't talk about how it will help ease your and your team's pain.

- They don't care about your pain.
- They don't care that what you're asking for is going to make you more efficient.
- They don't care that it's going to make your life easier.
- They don't care about retaining staff by avoiding burnout.

What they care about is their pain and how what you're asking for is going to benefit them.

So you have to couch it in terms of how it will make them look good and benefit the company or meet their other needs, which you better have determined before having this conversation.

From a corporate perspective, do talk about increased quality of creative services and how it will benefit sales. And do talk about speed to market and how that saves the company money.

No Problemo

It's very easy to fall into the trap of discussing the "buy" in terms of fixing something that's wrong with your team or the environment your team is operating in. Don't do this. It makes you look like you didn't plan well or, worse, that your manager didn't plan well—otherwise, the problem wouldn't have surfaced in the first place. Don't propose a solution to a problem, but rather talk about bringing more value and efficiency to your company/manager/client.

CHAPTER 6

The Master Plan: Intrapreneurialism

THE 50,000 FOOT VIEW

If you want the creative and professional freedoms enjoyed by your design firm and ad agency peers, you need to act like them and then some. The corporate environment is practically devoid of air for creatives and entrepreneurs. So strap on your oxygen tank and use this chapter as a guide on how to navigate the corporate landscape and build a self-sustaining creative ecosystem for you and your team.

It's easy for in-house teams to get lulled into a dangerous sense of complacency by having a guaranteed client base. Conversely, corporate design teams can get pounded into a self-defeating, passive-aggressive state of apathy by a dysfunctional corporate culture. You may think you can coast by on the policies mandated by upper management that force your clients to work with you and get lazy about marketing your team, improving your skills and focusing on customer service. Or you may be so abused by self-centered clients, unsupportive managers and inane and impassable corporate policies that you just give up, punch the time clock every morning, run out the door every evening and collect your paycheck. Either way, you and your team are at risk of disintegrating into the corporate ether.

Both scenarios leave you unfulfilled, compromised and at risk of a cynicism that will infect your personal and professional life. From what I've seen, there are only a few truly effective ways to address this malaise. One that I've witnessed to be a very powerful opportunity for positive change involves transforming your team by adopting a business model that has been in existence for over twenty years—intrapreneurialism. It is a paradigm, a philosophy, a structure that has been, ironically, adopted and embraced by the very business community that you're often struggling with. It's not new, and it's not groundbreaking. You may have already been putting into practice some of its key tenets. Rather than reinvent the wheel, you can leverage the credibility and validation associated with this model. It was conceived by respected business management gurus who your upper management may already be aware of.

Intrapreneurialism advocates setting up an entrepreneurial enterprise within the corporate environment. First coined in 1985 by Gifford Pinchot III, the idea was originally developed to be applied to internal R&D groups that were being smothered by bureaucratic and analytical initiatives. Pinchot argued that policies and procedures that worked for the management of corporate departments with fixed inputs and outputs, such as manufacturing, finance and operations, were not applicable to groups charged with innovation. These types of groups need flexibility and freedoms that corporations are often unwilling to grant.

In-house creative teams have the same function and needs as an R&D team, and the intrapreneurial paradigm is completely applicable to them. In-house groups, by the very nature of their mandate, have to be innovative. Their projects vary in scope and purpose, and the processes required to generate successful outcomes vary as well. Yet, as we all know, in-house groups are often held to the same strict corporate demands of standardization and compliance as teams with less demanding tasks and expectations. What's needed for creative services teams to succeed is the freedom to function as an entrepreneurial enterprise—as an agency or studio that happens to have only one corporation as its client.

> The path to becoming an intrapreneurial department is time and labor intensive, but the process is transformative and the rewards of personal and professional fulfillment are great.

It involves what I call the Four-Eyed Intrapreneurial Proposal: *investigation, ideation, implementation* and *integration*. In this chapter, I'll show you how to adopt this action plan and reposition your team using the intrapreneurial model.

As utopian as this may sound, it is absolutely achievable. R&D groups in companies ranging from high tech to financial services, including corporate giants such as 3M, Ford and DuPont, have successfully implemented this model.

This concept truly embodies the 50/50 proposition. You'll be straddling two worlds—one of creativity, freedom, and innovation and one of business plans, corporate politics and salesmanship. You'll need to develop and nurture relationships with internal advocates and create a business plan. You'll have to sell your plan in a way that resonates with the suits. Most importantly, you'll have to effect a fundamental shift in your own and your team's mindset and culture. You'll have to take ownership of your group. The moment you become an intrapreneur is the moment you stop looking at yourself as working for someone else. It is, in a very real sense, your agency now, with all the risks and rewards that come with that venture. The upside is you've got the corporation's resources at your disposal; the downside is you have to wrestle with the ingrained corporate culture to achieve your goals.

By adopting the intrapreneurial moniker, you'll have a leg up because you'll be advocating a known quantity to upper management. Taking the intrapreneurial action items and adapting them to your enterprise/vision will provide you with a structure that your business advocates and clients can relate to, and more importantly, you'll end up with specific strategies on staffing, billing, workflow and marketing that will take your team to the next level.

As they say in the corporate world, the net-net of what I'm getting at is that by being proactive and designing and implementing a business plan, you can achieve a business model that establishes your team as an ad agency or design firm within your company with all the opportunities and rewards that come with that structure.

So let's begin with the Four-Eyed Intrapreneurial Proposal: investigation, ideation, implementation and integration. Completing each of these steps is critical to your long-term success.

INVESTIGATION: KNOW THYSELF

In order to know where you want to go and who you want to be, it's essential to know where and who you are at the beginning of your journey. This may be hard to do. You may be so busy that you don't want to take the time or it may feel too disheartening and emotional to touch on. Regardless of these challenges and fears, just do it. Otherwise, all your efforts to improve your work life will, at best, result in tepid success and, at worst, put you in a less desirable place than you were when you began.

GREAT EXPECTATIONS

The most fundamental information you need to create your business plan is what you, your team, your clients and your company want to get out of the deal. In other words, what are everyone's expectations of each other and of the plan or initiative. These are the informal and often unstated contracts that exist for and within your team.

Specifically what are:

- all your expectations about the outcome of implementing the intraprenuerial business plan
- your expectations of your team
- your team's expectations of you
- your and your team's expectations of your clients
- your clients' expectations of you and your team
- your and your team's expectations of the company
- your company's expectations of you and your team

Once you have a sense of the answers to these questions, you'll understand what your goals are and who is in the best position to contribute to achieving those goals.

QUESTION MARKS

This section includes two surveys. One has a series of questions for you and your team to answer, the other is for your clients and colleagues in other departments to fill out. Both are designed to support you in your quest for self-definition and self-discovery. I'd encourage you to refine and adapt them to better address the unique circumstances in your company. As for delivery and implementation, you can present the questionnaires as hardcopy documents to fill out, e-mail them as a digital document or use a web-based solution such as Survey-Monkey to gather the data. Choose whichever route best suits your capabilities and then implement it. This tactic is critical to your success. If you're not committed to this process, then close this book now and use it as a doorstop or paperweight.

THE IN-HOUSE INTERNAL ASSESSMENT

Design Team Survey

Size of group:

Desired size of group:

Team positions (i.e., number of proofreaders, designers, project managers, etc.):

Desired structure:

Approximate number of projects per year:

Desired number of projects per year:

Annual billing:

Desired annual billing:

Do you charge back?
O Yes
O No

Do you track your billings?
O Yes
O No

What department does your team report to?

Desired department to report to:
Number of clients:
Desired number of clients:
Breakdown of projects by tier*: _____ % tier one _____ % tier two _____ % tier three
Desired projects by tier: _____ % tier one _____ % tier two _____ % tier three
Breakdown of projects by media: _____ % posters/signage _____ % interactive/web _____ % brochures _____ % sales aids _____ % newsletters _____ % internal forms

*Description of tiers:

- Tier one is the development and execution of initial creative work not based on prior project designs.
- Tier two is the repurposing of existing creative, such as adapting ad graphics to a brochure.
- Tier three includes minor edits or image revisions to existing files, usually referred to as production.

_____ % annual reports

_____ % packaging

_____ % ads

_____ % point of purchase

_____ % catalogs

_____ % branding

Company culture:

Team culture:

Are you and your team aligned with your company's mission?
O Yes
O No

Are you satisfied with your salary/compensation?
O Yes
O No

Rate your bureaucratic challenges:
O extremely difficult
O difficult
O manageable
O no challenges

List your three biggest challenges:

1.

2.

3.

List your three biggest assets:

1.

2.

3.

List your team's three greatest strengths:

1.

2.

3.

List your team's three greatest weaknesses:

1.

2.

3.

Do you utilize SOPs?
O Yes
O No

Do you use a project management software solution?
O Yes
O No

Do you use a DAM solution?
O Yes
O No

Rate overall quality of your client relationships:
- O excellent
- O good
- O satisfactory
- O poor

Rate team morale:
- O excellent
- O good
- O satisfactory
- O poor

Rate opportunities for strategic involvement in your company's marketing initiatives:
- O excellent
- O good
- O satisfactory
- O poor

Rate your team's overall business and business communications skills:
- O excellent
- O good
- O satisfactory
- O poor

Rate how you believe your clients perceive your service and value:
- O excellent
- O good
- O satisfactory
- O poor

Client Survey

Please rate your in-house creative team's overall quality of service:
- O excellent
- O good
- O satisfactory
- O poor

Please rate overall quality of deliverables:

    O excellent
    O good
    O satisfactory
    O poor

If allowed a choice, check which types of projects you would choose your in-house team over an agency for: (Check all that apply.)

    O production (revising existing design projects)
    O repurposing of existing materials (i.e., taking an ad and making it into a brochure)
    O initial creative

Were the deliverables:

Well designed?

    O always
    O most of the time
    O some of the time
    O never

Delivered on time?

    O always
    O most of the time
    O some of the time
    O never

Accurate (spelling, grammar, content)?

    O always
    O most of the time
    O some of the time
    O never

Successful at meeting the defined objectives?

    O always
    O most of the time
    O some of the time
    O never

Please rate overall quality of customer service:

- O excellent
- O good
- O satisfactory
- O poor

Were the department liaisons:

Polite?

- O always
- O most of the time
- O some of the time
- O never

Responsive?

- O always
- O most of the time
- O some of the time
- O never

Proactive?

- O always
- O most of the time
- O some of the time
- O never

Organized?

- O always
- O most of the time
- O some of the time
- O never

Knowledgeable?

- O always
- O most of the time
- O some of the time
- O never

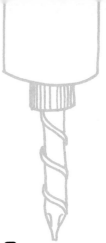

IDEATION: GOALS, STRATEGIES AND TACTICS

The most efficient way to create a business plan for your group is to use the goals/strategies/tactics process as your blueprint. This exercise allows you to establish your big picture aspirations and then methodically drill down to the specific action items that you and your team need to undertake to reach those goals.

The goals are your top-level objectives—what you want to achieve. Strategies are general statements of what needs to be done to achieve your goals—in other words, your plan. The tactics are the "in the trenches," "who does what by when" actions needed to forward your strategies.

Here's an example: Let's say you want to create best-in-class creative work. That's your broad goal. One of several strategies that you would probably want to implement is the recruiting of superior, highly talented designers. One tactic would most likely be for you or one of your team members to go to your local university's graduating design class portfolio showing to determine if there are any graduates worth considering for your team.

What follows are some issues specific to each of these steps that you should consider when creating your business plan.

GOALS: FALL INTO THE GAP

Look back to your design team survey. Hidden in that exercise are many of your goals. They exist in the gaps between your answers to where you actually are and your desired state. For example, you may see a significant difference between the tier one projects you're currently working on and the amount that you would like to work on. There is a ready-made goal: Increase tier one creative projects by X percent.

There are other gaps that may be a bit more painful to confront—those being the disconnect between your perception of the services you're providing and your clients' assessment of your team's performance. Granted, there may be political motives behind a client's rating, but more likely than not, you may have overestimated your effectiveness at meeting your clients' needs. Explore those gaps and establish relevant goals.

Work with your team to generate additional goals. They should, in some way, be tied into your company's goals and expectations of your department; build on your company's objectives but never subtract from them. Be sure to attach a broad timeframe to your goals.

Your objectives should be reasonable but challenging and, most importantly, true to your aspirations. They should force you to stretch and take you out of your comfort zone but not be so ambitious that you set yourself and your team up to fail. In addition to working with your team, reach out to internal sponsors, designers outside of your company and possibly consultants for objective suggestions, which are critical to generating appropriate goals. This is not an individual exercise. It's a team event.

It's very important to make sure your goals are quantifiable and that you establish the metrics necessary for measuring your success. This is an important tool that will allow you and your team to gauge the success of your strategies and tactics and determine if and when to change course. It's also critical to establishing your credibility and value with upper management. By being able to serve up hard data to the finance, opera-

tions, HR and C-level management teams, you will ensure their respect and continued support of your efforts.

INTERNAL STRATEGIES: THE CAR AND HOW IT RUNS

While you will be generating very specific strategies unique to your team's environment and goals, there are some broad issues to keep in mind. They range from staffing, marketing and infrastructure to securing sponsors. The strategies basically fall into two categories: internal strategies (what changes you need to make within your group); and external strategies (actions you and your team need to take to change the corporate environment—your clients, sponsors, peers, etc.—to achieve your goals). It's like going on a road trip. You have to make sure your car (the team) is tuned up and full of gas, the tires are inflated and the drivers are up for the trip, and you need to deal with the road (your company) by having maps, planned rest stops and places to stay.

Staffing

The vision you create for the kind of group you want and need to be will dictate your staffing structure. This is the fundamental issue to address before proceeding to any other strategy necessary to meet your goals. Refer to "Staffing Strategies" in chapter one for detailed ideas and options you'll need to explore to better craft your staffing strategies.

Standard Operating Procedures

Once you've designed your staffing structure, you'll need to determine the processes, procedures and policies that will best support your overall objectives. This part of the strategizing process will necessitate working with the key co-workers in other departments with whom you interact in the course of executing your projects. "Processing the Process Process" in chapter one should serve as a guide in creating your SOPs.

Infrastructure

The staff and SOPs you design will dictate your infrastructural needs. You'll need to determine what physical space will best support your team (cubes vs. open architecture; to embed or not to embed). Digital infrastructure and outside departmental support such as HR, operations, facilities and finance should also be included in this plan. See "Infrastructure: The House That Jack Built" in chapter one for background on this subject.

Finance

Finally, now that a coherent model has been developed for your group, you'll need to determine the most efficient means to fund it. Will you have an annual lump sum pulled from operations or administrative budgets to fund your group or will you create a chargeback system where your budget is actually funded by transferring money from your clients' budgets to yours. See "Show Me the Money: The In-House Cost Savings Rationale" in chapter three.

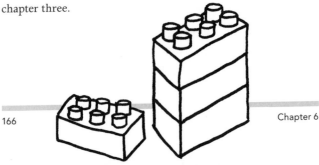

EXTERNAL STRATEGIES:
THE ROAD AND HOW TO NAVIGATE IT

Positioning Your Team

Using your vision for your team as a guide, you will need to understand your company's structure and choose the best position for your team within that structure that will allow you to achieve your objectives. Should your group be in the marketing, product development or even operations department? What level should the team be at? Where can you have the most freedom and greatest impact?

Advocates

This is the most important, external strategic plan you'll be creating. You will need to determine those in the company who are in the best position to support you in your efforts. Then you will have to choose the most effective means of enrolling them in your cause. This area may be the one with which you have the most difficulty as it will be the most political and Machiavellian of all your strategies. Chapter five can provide you with some insights that will help you in your efforts in securing reliable sponsors.

Marketing

You will need to market your group to various key stakeholders in a variety of ways. One crucial plan to keep in mind is the bottom-up, top-down strategy (see chapter three). By providing excellent customer service and deliverables to your clients, while effectively communicating your cost and performance efficiencies to upper management, you set the stage for a scenario where these two groups validate your value to each other, thus enhancing your position in the company.

TACTICS

Tactics are the "in the trenches," "who does what by when" action items that support your strategies. These actions may stretch your team but should not overwhelm you or them. The tactics often must be completed in addition to the work you're already doing. It can be a bit like building a plane while it's in flight. That means you should be realistic in your expectations and not set anyone up to fail.

If you hit hurdles, this is where you readjust and revise your plan—not at the level of goals, which should remain constant. It's like setting an endpoint for a trip full of detours and bad weather. You may be delayed and change your route because of rain, but your goal is to eventually get to your destination.

IMPLEMENTATION: BUILD IT AND THEY WILL COME

This is where the rubber meets the road, when you boot up and bang out the actions and tactics you've decided upon and kick butt and take names.

TEAM UP

Make sure that the people you've chosen to execute your tactics are appropriately matched to their assigned actions. Play to their strengths. This is not the time to develop your team. They need to be able to hit the ground running. If you have a small team assigned to developing SOPs, their design prowess is much less important than their organizational and analytical skills. Conversely, the designers working on your promotional efforts should be your best talent to showcase your team's creative abilities.

Make sure that your implementation team takes ownership of their roles and responsibilities and that they have a vested personal interest in their success. These people cannot be your clockers, the nine-to-fivers that are out the door when the second-hand hits the twelve. There will surely be instances when your implementation efforts are going to eat into personal time, and your team has to be willing to acknowledge and accept that fact.

Hold frequent status meetings. Not only does this keep everyone on track and coordinated in their efforts, but it also boosts morale. To that point, don't be afraid to take on a slightly subversive entrepreneurial attitude. If the goals and strategies are appropriate and you deal with others respectfully, there's nothing wrong with acting like a bit of a cowboy.

TAKE STRATEGIC RISKS

There is little in a corporate culture that supports entrepreneurial activity. Most organizations are built on conformity, standardization, consistency and strict procedures. Add to that peoples' natural aversion to change and you have an environment that is primed to oppose your every move.

The most frightening choices you'll be faced with are those that challenge existing policy and may put you at risk. If your goals are aligned with your company's goals and your actions are ethical and legal and do not put your company at risk, then

I'd advise you to go out on a limb and unilaterally take actions that challenge existing processes because there will be times when that will be the only way to achieve your objectives.

PLAN B: THE NEED FOR CONTINGENCIES

You can be sure that some of the tactics you work up will fail and that many of the situations you plan for will change. Hence, you need a plan B for every strategy and goal you set. If one of your strategies is to increase your group's annual budget and you're barred from implementing a chargeback system, look at establishing retainers with your clients or pulling your funding from marketing's budget instead of operations.' The point is not to abandon an objective but rather to find a different way to achieve it.

THE HOW (NOT JUST THE WHAT)

Creatives are not necessarily the most politically adept bunch. As such, it's especially important that the group that is going to be out there representing your team in what may be difficult or delicate situations be coached on how best to present themselves and their case for whatever request they are making.

Though much information and advice is provided in chapter five, nothing can replace common sense, emotional patience and team coaching and support. You also need to be strategic in who you choose to have which conversations with whom. If there is a crucial meeting with a VP, find the most articulate and strategic team member, regardless of her position in the department, and have her make the pitch. There may be times, if your budget permits, to bring in consultants to assist with this phase.

Though you will have established timelines, airtight tactics and a motivated team, you most likely will flounder and fall behind in your attempts to implement your plan.

> The most important ingredient for your success is commitment—a resolution to move forward regardless of the difficulties and setbacks you and your team will encounter.

I've never witnessed a failure when the creatives maintained an unwavering will to meet their goals. Upper management often recognizes and rewards resolve and focus. The fact that you take action, independent of what those actions are, will capture your company's attention and enhance your reputation.

Chapter 6

INTEGRATION: RE-EXAMINATION AND RENEWAL

Two key challenges remain once you've implemented your business plan—maintaining internal sustainability and growth and achieving external buy-in and integration.

THE LONG HAUL

If you make positive changes in procedures that, over time, start to fade and be ignored, all your hard-won gains in efficiency, stature and morale will be lost. It is much easier for a group of people to fall into undisciplined anarchy than maintain focus and good, but difficult, habits.

To avoid the deterioration of best business practices, you must put in place structures, processes and a culture that consistently reinforces individual behaviors and states of mind that support your group's objectives. This means scheduling procedural training and review seminars, creating and disseminating documents that powerfully reinforce key practices and promote positive perceptions of the group, and establishing means for every member of the team to take ownership of his own and the group's success.

This may be your most difficult task, for when the excitement of making revolutionary changes fades and the press of daily workload and challenges increases, no one will be inspired enough to add complexity or discipline to an already demanding environment. Without this discipline and commitment, though, all gains will be lost.

Always keep in mind that creatives tend to learn and respond to training differently than other more verbal- and process-centric staff. This means that the way you approach the reinforcement and addition of departmental policies and procedures should be tailored to your team's learning style. Employing clever tactics, such as goofy acronyms, playful manuals and visual metaphors, will have a better chance of being absorbed and adopted than drier clinical documents filled with flowcharts and bullet points.

BUILD IT AND MAKE SURE THEY COME

As stated earlier, people, especially in a corporate setting, are naturally resistant to change—even if it greatly improves their company. While you may have achieved your goals, there is no long-term chance for survival and growth without real buy-in from every group in your company. Some departments may have had your services forced upon them and will be looking for ways to ensure that you fail even though your success benefits the company as a whole. Others will have to take on extra responsibilities and blame your team for the additional workload. It is therefore up to you to smooth over resentments and build and nurture long-term relationships with other departments in your company.

Nothing helps enroll others in your long-term success better than the establishment and maintenance of personal relationships. You need to go out of your way to get to know your peers in the departments with whom you interact and rely upon.

Casual visits and lunches and more formal planned inclusion in key departmental meetings and initiatives will help bring important and necessary allies into the fold.

Changing the way your team operates will necessitate integrating your new enterprise into the existing corporate structures and processes. This exercise will be logistical, such as working with finance to establish a chargeback system or aligning with marketing on strategies for working together.

An important tool in establishing these procedures is to incorporate assessments and reviews into your partnerships with key departments. This serves two purposes. First, it lets your peers know that you are serious about and committed to the establishment of efficient and sustainable partnerships with them. Second, it gives you the information you need to create and refine the policies and procedures necessary for those successful partnerships.

READ THE METER: ESTABLISH METRICS FOR SUCCESS

The creation and continual refinement of metrics by which you can measure your team's success is the final piece of the

intrapreneurial model that needs to be established. Unless you know how well your team is performing and why, you will be unable to adapt to your ever-changing corporate environment. You will then need to continually change to meet the new challenges and opportunities you're presented with. Whether this involves restructuring your team, adopting new policies and procedures or redefining your mission, the "adapt or die" adage is especially applicable to internal creative teams.

CHAPTER 7

The In-House
Strategy,
In Conclusion

THE SECRET OF SERVICE

This chapter covers various topics relevant to the practice of in-house design that either were not touched upon in the other chapters of this book or that reinforce key ideas discussed earlier. All address uncomfortable or overlooked—but important—subjects with the objective of encouraging dialogue within our vibrant and growing community.

As creatives immersed in the often restrictive conservative corporate culture of their host companies, designers tend to reflexively react to their environment by either rebelling and asserting their artistic persona or succumbing to corporate culture and assimilating so completely that they forsake their creative innovative spirits. Often, they vacillate wildly between the two. I know I have. One minute, I'll be donning my khakis and Oxford shirts, boning up on my corporate speak for a big presentation, and the next, I'll be getting my ear pierced and lamenting my clients' bad taste and lack of marketing savvy.

The only way I've found to avoid these often counterproductive and inappropriate extremes is to focus on what I am trying to accomplish and how I'm trying to accomplish it—in other words, how I can best serve my company. It is only then that I maintain my objectivity and act in an authentic and appropriate manner. It's all about focus, helping others in achieving corporate goals and avoiding the distraction of ego and image. Achieving and maintaining this state of mind and culture of service requires a great deal of discipline.

Below are some red flags signaling you're on the path to becoming a corporate pod-person or have given up accountability and entered a state of resignation. Beware of the following thoughts:

- If it's in the manual, it must be right.
- That's the way we've always done it.
- My peers are experts; they must know what they're talking about.
- Human resources says it's okay.
- The company is always looking out for my (and my team's) best interests.
- If I rock the boat, I'll get fired.
- If you're a VP, you must be good at what you do.
- I'll just lay low, hunker down and everything will be okay.
- I'll be appreciated and rewarded if I do a good job.
- It's not my job.
- My clients have to use me.
- My clients need to adapt to my business model.

Here's the other extreme, where you're all about ego and personal gain:

- No one appreciates me.
- My clients are morons.
- I know more about marketing than my clients do.
- I'm too talented to be working here.
- It's not my job.
- My clients have to use me.
- My clients need to adapt to my business model.

(Paradoxically, the last three bullets show up in both mindsets.)

> Whichever extreme you're experiencing at any given moment, know that you're in a bad place and that you need to change your conversation.

So, what is the best new conversation to adopt? I'd recommend, "How can I help? How can I best serve the company?" Brad Weed, creative director at Microsoft, considers it a bit differently. He looks for where he and his team can have the greatest impact. When all is said and done, he searches for situations outside of his defined role for ways he and his team can contribute to and support Microsoft, be it giving graphic form to complex ideas or reviewing ad campaigns for new product releases.

I hope you'll be able to get past the Pollyanna overtones of the service phrase and look at the value it can bring to you, your co-workers and your company. If your focus is on how you can help, you'll be looking objectively at ways to improve your and your company's situation, leading to a better, more successful and healthier work environment. Who's going to argue with that?

Adopting this mantra can take you to some interesting places beyond the usual creative services you provide for your company. It's entirely possible, for example, that you begin to leverage your expertise in providing PDFs—and in the creative review process to propose and design marketing routing and approval solutions. If you provide copywriting and proofreading to your clients, you may expand into transcription services. Your print buying could evolve into bringing short-run digital services in-house.

Whatever direction you take, with service to your company as a guiding principle, it will surely be a path to success.

THE Q FACTOR

There's a word that is slowly, insidiously being erased from the collective vocabulary of companies and the in-house design community that serves them: quality. Once this ideal is negated as a defining force in your company, your clients will begin to spurn quality, which is the fundamental essence of design. The value of design is then diminished and erroneously considered to be subjective and unquantifiable. Your clients will just want to get the job done and out the door as quickly and cheaply as possible. In spite of this perception, as designers, we know quality is integral to effective design.

So, how do you communicate, institute and embed the value quality brings to a company in the guise of good design?

That process begins with a series of acts that coincidentally are as dependent on quality execution as the design work your team produces. Those tactics include the development of rich, quality relationships with clients, peers and upper management;

the creation of a quality work environment; and finally, the choosing and nurturing of quality talent.

Q-RELATIONSHIPS

I'd like to take a moment to relate a personal story in the hope of enhancing the quality of this essay. My sixteen-year-old daughter is learning disabled. By most quantitative measures, which she's exhaustively been tested for, she is functioning at a below-average level. It never ceases to strike me though, when "experts," who previously only knew her through the reports they've read, are taken aback by her humor, poise and creativity upon meeting her in person. They experience the quality, not the quantity, of her being.

The same happens to corporate creatives. Quantified on a financial spreadsheet, we appear as liabilities to our companies, a profit drain, a necessary evil. Stereotyped by corporate management, it's assumed we're flakey and overly emotional, lacking any business sensibilities. But in reality, in person, our value quickly becomes obvious. The creativity, resourcefulness and focus we bring to our endeavors will never show up in Excel. That's why it's so important for us not to hide from the harshness of corporate politics, but rather, dive into the fray.

As a corporate creative, you should seize (and create) opportunities to join in on strategic meetings regarding your projects. Aside from the obvious benefit of providing input that will make your job easier at the design stage, actively participating gives you a chance to strut your creative and strategic know-how.

Too often, it's assumed that designers are just needed to implement others' ideas. In addition to speaking up in meetings, designers can also express ideas to clients through e-mails and also by presenting concepts outside the communicated direction that speak to new and innovative strategic options. Independently, conducting post mortems and sharing them with clients communicates a level of quality thinking that demonstrates the value creatives bring beyond just making pretty images. Cite studies on the value of design; create white papers comparing good and bad design solutions and the value good design brings to a company.

Finally, it's critical that you form personal relationships with your clients and upper management. Time and again, I've witnessed and heard stories that validate this suggestion. Without a bond more substantial than procedural interaction, there is no trust. Without trust, there is no opportunity to create a level of belief in our abilities to make the right choices in the execution of our projects. Without that belief, there is no freedom to bring quality and value to your contributions in the process of creating powerful design solutions for your company.

Q-WORK ENVIRONMENT

Creating a quality working environment is difficult, but necessary, for enhancing the quality of your work. At the bare minimum, requiring creative briefs (or job orders for simpler projects) is a must. Creating basic schedules defining the who, what, where and when is critical. Finally, keeping a constant flow of communication with clients that is clear and concise will ensure the successful execution of your projects and will demonstrate the quality of your professionalism.

There may be little ability to control your physical space, but, again, there are some reasonable minimum requirements you need to insist on. Your teams should be physically clustered together, preferably with a common meeting area. You need current software and hardware and appropriate art supplies. Bandwidth, Internet access and ample storage infrastructure is critical to the quality performance of your day-to-day tasks.

Q-TALENT

More important than any needs outlined so far is assembling a team of quality talent. Positions in other groups are much more forgiving of mediocrity than those on a creative team. It's one

thing to find accountants who can add and subtract and understand basic accounting practices; it's entirely another thing to settle for a designer who doesn't understand how to effectively bring marketing direction to the design of his assignments. Acquiring this level of quality talent is difficult for in-house teams who are competing with ad agencies and design studios for staff. You must secure budgets that allow for competitive wages, offer challenging career opportunities and provide for peer acknowledgment. Entering design contests that showcase the level of work produced by your teams is a good step towards self-promotion that will resonate with potential candidates. Press releases, creative team websites and networking at industry events are also critical to engaging quality talent to recruit for your department.

BEWARE THE C-FACTOR

In addition to all these recommendations, make sure that whatever you do, you never fall into the mindset that promotes the C-factor, a.k.a. commodity. As soon as you do, you strip away the value you bring to your company and the quality of

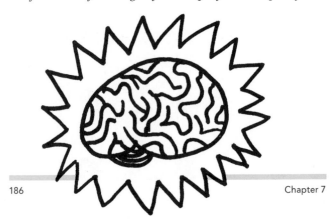

your working life as a designer. Corporate life then becomes all about doing things faster and cheaper. This paradigm assumes that you, your skills, your strengths and your job are the same as everyone else's and that the only distinguishing feature between you and an agency, a co-worker or a potential new hire is cost. It devalues your life and your individuality. It ignores all the unique skills and traits you have to offer.

> Don't ever view yourself or the work you provide as a commodity—something that can be bought or traded—a position on an organizational chart. You are an individual with unique gifts and talents.

THE Q IMPERATIVE

If you don't effectively advocate for quality in your companies, you and your team are destined to become mere order takers with fixed inputs and outputs, devoid of quality thought and design, that add no real value to your company. Conversely, if you are successful, you garner respect for yourself and your peers that will result in an inspiring working environment, professional fulfillment and opportunities to powerfully further your company's mission.

PROCUREMENT:
THE KEYS TO THE KINGDOM

One of the last places a creative team might think to go for help is purchasing or procurement, yet there is no other department that more powerfully has your team's fate in their hands and thus is more able to help you.

Procurement departments are all about efficiency and cost-savings—values that many of your clients may not share. Clients want ease of use and expediency. They want a vendor who will do their job for them in addition to providing good creative work. Therefore, they turn to outside profit-driven resources that are all too happy to take on additional roles and, of course, charge a pretty penny for them.

How often have you witnessed agencies providing creative briefs, marketing plans and project management for their clients in addition to the creative services they were originally contract-ed for? Rush jobs because the client sat on the project too long? —

Not a problem. Incomplete or undecipherable job order? —Piece of cake. Ridiculous workload for no money because of improper budgeting? —We'll make it up on the next job.

To be fair, many clients require this level of service because they are overworked and understaffed. No matter where the blame falls, though, the company loses if agencies are used for the wrong reasons and it's procurement's mandate to plug the holes in the budget dike. Your team is in the best position to fill those gaps. If your friends in purchasing don't know that, then you should step up and elucidate them on the value you can and do bring in supporting the marketing department.

Purchasing's culture is probably radically different from yours, so you will have to adapt your style of communication to bridge that divide by adopting a business style that is objective, detail-oriented and all about savings.

> You'll need to do your homework in order to create spreadsheets that document the potential savings your team can offer your company.

It will also be important to carefully and patiently explain what services you and your company's agency partners provide, how you provide them and the costs associated with those services. This might include assisting purchasing in deciphering agency invoices to ensure that a comparative cost analysis is accurate.

As the purchasing department comes to trust and even rely on your expertise, your team could end up supporting them with their agency reviews and contracts. It goes without saying that you should be forthright and realistic in how your team can best service your company and when it would be appropriate to use agencies to meet your corporation's needs.

The best scenario for your success is one where purchasing tactfully prods reluctant clients to use your team. If their political skills are lacking, you should assertively advocate for a more carrot and less stick approach. Mandates often backfire. Clients don't like to be backed into a corner, especially with an initiative that may make their lives harder, and they may be inclined to sabotage the effort. It's much better if the relationship builds incrementally with baby steps that afford your clients some sense of control and give your team time to surprise them with your agency level of service.

> So, shake hands with the number crunchers and take them out to lunch—low budget, of course.

A SERVANT OF TWO MASTERS

It's important to remember that creating a productive and sustainable team requires you to be a servant of two masters. On one hand, you and your fellow creatives need to meet your company's expectation that you create high-quality deliverables as efficiently, quickly and cost effectively as possible.

The other side of this equation, the one often neglected out of fear or browbeating by upper management and the bean counters, is your obligation to yourself and your team.

> Is your work environment healthy and sustainable?

Does it allow for a modicum of self-expression, flexibility in process and inspirational exercises and opportunities? Is the workload manageable? Do you have the resources and tools necessary for the execution of your responsibilities? If the answer is no, then you need to take action to have any, and all, of these issues addressed.

You may be inclined to deal with difficult and counterproductive situations subversively or passive-aggressively, but those behaviors obviously will not improve your situation and will damage your standing within your company. This leaves you in the uncomfortable position of openly challenging established policies that many believe are in the best interests of the company, but which you know are not.

> The rationale here goes beyond ROI. The issues are about the ethical, humane and proper treatment of your staff.

This may sound like hyperbole, but there are many organizations that fall into such a deep state of insular self-centered culture that people come to accept the unacceptable.

In addition to ethical considerations, there are also financial repercussions when teams are improperly managed. A group that is overworked, underpaid, assigned responsibility without authority, given unachievable goals and little logistical or moral support will under perform and wither, costing their companies money as a result of their poor productivity.

It is your job to document the problems and make a reasoned, objective case for change to the highest appropriate levels of management. If you do not get the response you need, then you can either challenge the company in a venue outside of the company through legal means, or you can leave.

As mentioned earlier, your other obligation is, of course, to your company. Unfortunately, many in-house creative teams forget the unwritten agreement between them and their employer, which is to provide the best creative services to their companies that they are capable of.

Too often, internal groups come to think of their employment as a right, not a privilege, leading to a mindset of entitlement that impacts their commitment to their jobs. The guarantee of steady work, the bureaucratic cultures of other departments and a false sense of value all contribute to a detrimental mindset of "What's in it for me?" rather than "How can I help?"

Your two masters: (1) the company and their goals, and (2) you, your team and your goals. You need a balance to ensure sustainability. Meet outward needs. Meet inward needs.

THE CUSTOMER
IS ALWAYS RIGHT

In-house is retail. There is the deliverable that is either tangible, a printed document, for example; or intangible, such as design and brand consulting. Then there is the customer service component. Both are equally important in determining the success of your team, and one should never be confused with the other.

> Simply providing great creative services is not all that is expected or required of in-house teams, though it may be easy and preferable for designers to believe that. It is not a substitute for good customer service.

If you walk into a high-end clothing store that is selling the most fashionable, well-made clothing known to man and your salesperson is oppositional, inarticulate and arrogant, you'll leave without buying a thing. The same holds true for in-house teams who are "selling" their designs and services to their clients. If they provide great creative but treat their clients poorly, their clients will rebel regardless of the creative work.

Agencies, being more entrepreneurial enterprises, understand the importance of customer relations. In-house teams, with a seemingly guaranteed workflow, tend to get lulled into a false sense of security, believing that they are immune to their customers walking away from their business. Any team that adopts this mindset is in peril of losing business to outside agencies and being dissolved, while perpetuating the stereotype of the designer as a rebellious individualistic prima donna who is unwilling to be a team player.

It's easy for creatives, even those who understand the value of customer service, to struggle and deal inappropriately with difficult clients and unmanageable corporate bureaucracy out of fear that they may be devaluing design by providing what could be considered good customer service. The default response may be to just say "no," complain about a lack of respect or punish their clients for their admittedly poor behavior. The mistaken belief is that by making these demands, clients are exhibiting their lack of respect and appreciation of design. This may or may not be true, but it is a poor use of a creative team's time to dwell on this question. What is true is that these clients are definitely showing that they do not understand the process of design, and it is in the creative team's best interest to educate their clients on the process and any fixed needs they have rather than adopt an oppositional stance.

Creatives need to be careful not to use their clients' ignorance of the design process as an excuse to provide poor customer service. Designers actually should embrace customer service as a critical function. This means putting aside frustrations over clients' unreasonable demands and objectively looking for ways to meet or mitigate those demands.

> That being said, your client is not your final customer—the corporation is. If you believe the client is not acting, either intentionally or unintentionally, in the best interests of your company, you are obligated to take a reasoned and objective stand.

What behaviors, functions and activities actually fall under the moniker of customer service? Certainly meeting difficult deadlines, fielding multiple revisions, and providing services outside of the design function, such as copywriting, proofreading and procurement, are part of the mix. But your mindset is equally as important. A can-do, "whatever it takes" attitude, coupled with a complete commitment to tackling any and all problems as they present themselves will cement your reputation as the go-to team for your clients.

BRAND BLINDNESS

I'm at our New York showroom meeting with John, the creative director from the licensing division of a major entertainment conglomerate, to discuss the packaging for the introduction of an antique version of a well-known cartoon character. John's passion for the character is inspiring, and I'm hoping that the designs I'll be responsible for will meet his expectations. Halfway into the conversation, he locks me in his gaze and declares, "For the packaging to work, you have to be the character!" Whoa—for a second I feel like I'm in a Lee Strasberg acting class. I take his impassioned advice to heart and create an award-winning box, but the product fails in the marketplace.

Jump eight years later. My company's senior VP of sales, our marketing analyst and I are discussing a sub-brand of our baby line. Named M.V.B., for Most Valuable Baby, it's a line of sports-themed infant items. The VP asks me what I think of the name and the trade dress. I tell him I think it's clever and that new fathers would be attracted to the sports-like graphics my team has created for the packaging and point-of-purchase. Very diplomatically, they disagree.

There are three key points to their rationale. First, our company's primary purchasers are female and too masculine a display design may turn them off to the product. Second, most women probably wouldn't get that the M.V.B. moniker is a play off the sports abbreviation M.V.P.—Most Valuable Player. Finally, there may be resistance from the retailer to placing a display and packaging with a primary color palette in their basically pastel retail environment.

I put aside my ego and acknowledge the validity of these arguments. I also realize that I've been guilty of something I instinctively responded to eight years earlier in my meeting with John—brand blindness. Let me explain.

I define brand blindness as the tunnel vision that results from a creative being too close to the product, message and culture of a company. Especially vulnerable are in-house designers who end up forming unrealistic assumptions about how their company, its product and its services are perceived by the public, leading to flawed strategy and design. Another result of this affliction is that these same designers tend to abandon research, ignore their audience and create designs that are an homage to their brand, not a successful leveraging of it.

John's near fanatical devotion to his brand has resulted in huge successes for his company. Under his watchful eye, the quality and consistency of the product and packaging has been excellent. But in his and his company's zeal to create the perfect brand, they've often forgotten the wants and needs of their audience, and many product lines have missed the mark and failed as a result.

As an in-house creative, I, too, eat, breathe and live my company's brand. There are obvious advantages to this when I or my team set out to develop a new design that represents our company to the public. Less obvious are the pitfalls I mentioned above. In order to address this problem, our team has adopted a previous presidential campaign slogan with a slight change as our motto—"It's the customer, stupid!"

Specifically we now ask a set of questions before starting any new project:

- Who buys the product?
- Where is the first point of contact made?
- Is the brand message clearly communicated in the design?

Though these are obvious criteria to establish before taking on any project, our brand blindness has forced us to be more rigorous and disciplined in addressing these issues.

Ironically, when we started asking these questions, we found that not only had we been jumping to conclusions about our audience, but we had been making fatally flawed assumptions about our brand as well. When we evaluated our counter displays, we saw that we had actually been giving too little real estate to our logo. In inflating the importance of our brand, we mistakenly kept the logo smaller because we felt it was so powerful it didn't need to be that large. In looking at the point of contact, we also saw that our displays were lost in a sea of product in poorly designed retail environments, further diminishing any brand presence we had in that retail environment. Our team undertook working on a consistent trade dress to improve our brand's visual presence in the marketplace.

There are numerous other examples of how I've been a victim of brand blindness, but the main point I believe that needs to be stressed is that we all have to be aware that we harbor assumptions about our brands. What's obvious to us about our brand's attributes may very well be hidden from the consumer, and creating self-indulgent tributes to our brands is a surefire way to miss the mark in connecting with them. Questioning each project, its audience and its objectives is the best way for us in-house designers to beat brand blindness and "see the light."

IN·HOUSE IN·TEGRATION

It often seems as if upper management and clients see the design process as a simple affair where designers make a few sketches, push a few buttons and, violá!, a printed piece is magically delivered to them. We, of course, know that belief to be fantasy and utterly false. In actuality, the steps involved in taking a project from start to finish require numerous people with different areas of expertise, many of whom are not designers, to contribute to the workflow. They can include account executives, project managers, traffic coordinators, proofreaders, art buyers, print specialists and distribution coordinators—and that's not even including outside vendors.

This obvious fact speaks to the need for an integrated and coordinated approach to the production of your marketing, communication, and educational printed and digital deliverables. Ideally, all of these teams would report into a single head of a creative/marketing services department. By being held accountable to the same managers, these groups can avoid the infighting, turf wars and finger pointing that can occur when teams involved in the creative process have differing, and sometimes conflicting, goals and mandates.

A perfect (and often recounted) example of a workflow breakdown is the conflict that arises when files are handed off from one team to another. The design team complains that the project information given to them by the account team is inaccurate or incomplete. The production team is frustrated that the design team hands off sloppy, half-baked files to them, adding time and difficulty to their jobs. The print specialists receive incomplete color breaks and printing specs from the production team. And on and on and on.

Unfortunately, many departments accept this as an unavoidable fact of life and do little or nothing to effectively address it. Yet focusing on this problem can yield amazing efficiencies while improving morale and team relations.

If you are one of the fortunate few whose structure incorporates all of the noted groups in one department, then there is a clear path to improving the coordination between the groups in your department.

> Creating cross-functional teams that have the same goals and leaders is the surest way to guarantee that all efforts are coordinated and effective.

Barring that, departmental efforts where the heads of each of the functional teams present a unified front will go a long way towards cross-functional integration.

If your creative, production and distribution teams report into different departments, then integration must be addressed at both the upper and functional levels of your teams. Managers of the different teams will need to reach out and coordinate their efforts and look for ways to tie their individual team goals and successes to each other. If your corporation uses an annual goal-setting process to establish performance metrics for individuals and teams, use that process as the path toward creating common objectives that link various teams together.

On the functional level, frequent contact and the building of personal relationships will go a long way toward affecting cross team support. It's a lot harder to dump a project on someone you're friends with and see every day than an anonymous co-worker whom you can hide from.

Your projects will only be as good as the relationships between the different teams responsible for their execution. Without that, your team's performance will be hostage to your weakest link.

EPILOGUE

THE GIFTS YOU BRING

Ever been in a room full of adults and have a group of happy children come tumbling in? Have you noticed how the tenor in the room changes, becomes lighter, more joyful, more playful? Ever walked through the halls of a corporation past rows and rows of people pounding away at keyboards, piles of papers, folders, manuals, milestone calendars, to-do lists and day planners all crammed into their tiny impersonal spaces, and then come upon the creative department with their toy action figure collections, MoMA posters, colorful glowing monitors, playful banter, personal art, Photoshopped send-ups of their peers, Pantone books and piles of concept thumbnails bursting out of their cubes, designed in vain to impose some sense of order?

Malcolm Gladwell, in his seminal book, *The Tipping Point*, discusses how subtle changes in a group's environment can have profound effects on the culture of that group and how behaviors are contagious. I propose that our creative tribe can powerfully and positively alter the very fabric of the corporations that we work for.

So, be clear that the artifacts you create for your company are only a part of the gifts you bring to them. Dare I say that your creativity, entrepreneurship, playfulness, inquisitiveness, refusal to accept the status quo and respect for process (albeit a chaotic one) can inform and transform the way your company functions.

> Be smart, be passionate, be disciplined and be bold, but most of all, be true to who you are.

That is the greatest gift you can give to your company, to your fellow creatives and, most importantly, to yourselves.

INDEX